Spiritual Interview with
MARTIN LUTHER KING, JR.
American Problem And Dream

キング牧師 天国からのメッセージ
アメリカの課題と夢

大川隆法
Ryuho Okawa

本霊言は、2016年8月24日、幸福の科学 教祖殿 大悟館にて、
公開収録された(写真上・下)。

キング牧師 天国からのメッセージ
―アメリカの課題と夢―

Spiritual Interview with Martin Luther King, Jr.
— American Problem and Dream —

Preface

Here is God's Love.
Here is God's Truth.
Here is the Destiny of America.
These words are spoken as a symbol of
Voices from Heaven.

Through God's Eyes,
There can be seen Real Justice.
This is the Book of Justice.
A historical figure,
Well-known Martin Luther King, Jr. "spoke a lot."
No, "speaks a lot."
Believe his voice, and "One day,"
You'd be awakened by God Himself.

Sep. 15, 2016

Master Ryuho Okawa

はじめに

ここに神の愛あり。
ここに神理あり。
ここにアメリカの運命あり。
言の葉が紡がるるは象徴なり。
天から降りたる声なるがゆえに。

神の眼に見透かされては、
真の正義、現れざるはなし。
これなるは正義の書なり。
歴史にそそり立つ一人の偉人、
知らぬ人なきマルチン・ルーサー・キングJr.は
"多くを語りき。"
否、"いまも多くを語る。"
彼の声を信ぜよ、さすれば"いつの日か"、
あなたを目覚めさせようと揺さぶっているのが、
神御自身だと気づくだろう。

2016年9月15日
あなたがたの師　大川隆法

Contents

Preface 2

1 Martin Luther King, Jr. Talks About His Destiny 14
   Guided by God's order and God's love 24
2 Faith, Courage and Justice 30
   The power of Jesus' Father that is here now 32
   King heard the voice of God that is beyond human
   justice 38
3 Slavery, Discrimination and War 46
   White people have not reflected upon their history of
   slavery 48
   The next American president must apologize to Japan
   about the atomic bombings 52
   Vietnam War, Gulf War, and Iraq War 58
4 Solve Poverty and Immigration Issues by Providing
   Equal Chances 66
   America should be the champion of the countries of
   chances 68

目　次

はじめに 3

1 キング牧師、自らの運命を語る 15
　「神の命(めい)」と「神の愛」に導かれて 25

2 信仰、勇気そして正義 31
　今も世にある「イエスの父」の力 33
　人間的正義を超える「神の声」を聞いた 39

3 奴隷制度、人種差別、戦争 47
　白人は奴隷制度についての反省ができていない 49

　次の米大統領は日本に原爆投下を謝罪すべき 53

　ベトナム戦争、湾岸戦争、イラク戦争 59

4 貧困と移民問題は「チャンスの平等」で解決を 67

　アメリカはチャンスの国のチャンピオンであれ 69

	Government should provide equal conditions to the minority 76
	Black people are also humans with souls and intelligence 80
5	On Sexual Discrimination and Gun Control 86
	King's stance on the gender issue 86
	Solve gun control issue by learning from Japan 94
6	Terrorism and the U.S. Presidential Election 98
	A bridge is needed between the religious philosophies of America and the Middle East 100
	"America First" vs. "Lady First" 106
7	The Secret of Dr. King's Soul 112
	Past life is a person in the Old Testament 112
	"I invited my death" 120
	Friends in Heaven 124
8	A New Dream for America and the World 128
	After receiving the spiritual messages 132

* This spiritual interview was conducted in English. The Japanese text is a translation added by the Happy Science International Editorial Division.

政府は弱者にも「平等な条件」を提供せよ ……………… 77

　　黒人も人間であり、魂があり知能がある ……………… 81

5　**性差別と銃規制について** ……………… 87
　　ジェンダー問題に関するキングの見解 ……………… 87
　　銃社会の問題は日本に学んで解決を ……………… 95

6　**テロと米大統領選について** ……………… 99
　　米国と中東の宗教思想には「橋渡し」が必要 ……………… 101

　　「アメリカ・ファースト」vs.「レディー・ファースト」……… 107

7　**キング牧師の魂の秘密** ……………… 113
　　過去世は旧約聖書中の人物 ……………… 113
　　「私の死は自ら招いたもの」 ……………… 121
　　天上界での友人たち ……………… 125

8　**アメリカと世界の新たな夢** ……………… 129
　　霊言を終えて ……………… 133

※本書は、英語で収録された霊言に和訳を付けたものです。

This book is the transcript of spiritual messages given by Martin Luther King, Jr.

These spiritual messages were channeled through Ryuho Okawa. However, please note that because of his high level of enlightenment, his way of receiving spiritual messages is fundamentally different from other psychic mediums who undergo trances and are completely taken over by the spirits they are channeling.

It should be noted that these spiritual messages are opinions of the individual spirits and may contradict the ideas or teachings of the Happy Science Group.

本書は、キング牧師の霊言を収録したものである。

　「霊言現象」とは、あの世の霊存在の言葉を語り下ろす現象のことをいう。これは高度な悟りを開いた者に特有のものであり、「霊媒現象」（トランス状態になって意識を失い、霊が一方的にしゃべる現象）とは異なる。

　ただ、「霊言」は、あくまでも霊人の意見であり、幸福の科学グループとしての見解と矛盾する内容を含む場がある点、付記しておきたい。

Spiritual Interview with Martin Luther King, Jr.
— American Problem and Dream —

August 24, 2016

Master's Holy Temple: Sacred Shrine of Great Enlightenment, Taigokan

Happy Science, Tokyo

Spiritual Messages from Martin Luther King, Jr.

キング牧師 天国からのメッセージ
―アメリカの課題と夢―

2016年8月24日　東京都・幸福の科学　教祖殿　大悟館にて
キング牧師の霊言

Martin Luther King, Jr. (1929-1968)

An American Baptist minister and leader of the African-American Civil Rights Movement. Studied at Morehouse College, Crozer Theological Seminary, and Boston University. King planned and led the Montgomery bus boycott and the March on Washington, giving major influence to the Civil Rights Movement. He is renowned for his speeches, "I Have a Dream" and "I've Been to the Mountaintop." Inspired by the philosophies of Mahatma Gandhi, the leader of Indian independence, King committed himself to a movement of nonviolence and reconciliation. Won the Nobel Peace Prize in 1964. Assassinated on April 4, 1968 in Memphis, Tennessee. Received posthumous awards including the Presidential Medal of Freedom in 1977 and the Congressional Gold Medal in 2004.

Interviewers from Happy Science

Yuta Okawa

> Managing Director, Deputy Chief of CEO's Office
> Religious Affairs Headquarters, Advisor of General Headquarters,
> Activity Promotion Strategist of Political Headquarters,
> Activity Promotion Strategist of International Headquarters

Kazuhiro Ichikawa

> Senior Managing Director
> Chief Director of International Headquarters

Masashi Ishikawa

> Director General of International Editorial Division

※ The professional titles represent the position at the time of the interview.

マーティン・ルーサー・キング・ジュニア（1929 − 1968)

アメリカのバプテスト派牧師・アフリカ系アメリカ人公民権運動指導者。モアハウス大学、クローザー神学校、ボストン大学に学ぶ。モンゴメリー・バス・ボイコット運動やワシントン大行進など、公民権運動に大きな影響を与える運動を企画・指導。また、「I Have a Dream（私には夢がある）」「I've Been to the Mountaintop（私は山頂に達した）」などの演説で有名。インド独立の父マハトマ・ガンジーの思想に大きく影響を受け、非暴力で融和的な運動方針を貫いた。1964年、ノーベル平和賞を受賞。1968年4月4日、テネシー州メンフィスで暗殺された。死後、大統領自由勲章（1977年）、議会名誉黄金勲章（2004年）を受章。

質問者（幸福の科学）

大川裕太（幸福の科学常務理事　兼　宗務本部総裁室長代理　兼　総合本部アドバイザー　兼　政務本部活動推進参謀　兼　国際本部活動推進参謀）

市川和博（幸福の科学専務理事　兼　国際本部長）

石川雅士（国際編集局長）

※役職は収録当時のもの。

1 Martin Luther King, Jr. Talks About His Destiny

Kazuhiro Ichikawa Today, we would like to receive spiritual messages from Dr. Martin Luther King, Jr. entitled, "American Problem and Dream." But before that, today's spiritual message marks Master's 100th lecture in English. So, let's give our sincere gratitude. Congratulations!

Audience [*Applaud.*]

Ryuho Okawa Thank you. Good morning, everyone.

Audience Good morning.

Ryuho Okawa Today, I'd like to invite the spirit of Dr. Martin Luther King, Jr. Of course, he's very famous even in Japan because of his Civil Rights Movement,

1　キング牧師、自らの運命を語る

市川和博　本日はマーティン・ルーサー・キング・ジュニア牧師より、「アメリカの課題と夢」と題して霊言をいただきたいと思います。その前に、本日の霊言をもちまして総裁先生による「１００回目の英語御説法」となりますことに、心より感謝を捧げたいと思います。おめでとうございます。

（会場、拍手）

大川隆法　ありがとう。みなさん、おはようございます。

会場　おはようございます。

大川隆法　今日は、マーティン・ルーサー・キング・ジュニア牧師の霊をお招きしたいと思います。この方は、もちろん日本でも、公民権運動でたいへん有名です。黒人解放

which means the emancipation of black people. At that time, they were called Negroes. Now, we cannot use the word, "Negro." We use "black people." He left a trace that was very huge and very inspiring, and he, himself, lived an American dream. He was well known as the speaker of the "I Have a Dream" speech. When he led a great march, at that time, he said that the day will come when his little children can be friends with white children.

And this very short speech brought a gigantic reaction around the world. People were thinking about civil rights, and he himself, I mean Pastor

運動ですね。当時は黒人は「ニグロ」と呼ばれていました。現在はその言葉は使うことができなくなっており、"black people"（黒人）という言葉を使います。偉大な足跡を遺した方で、大きな感化を与え、自らアメリカン・ドリームを描いてみせた方でもあります。「I Have a Dream（私には夢がある）」という演説をした人として有名です。大行進を行ったとき、彼は、いつの日か、自分の子供たちと白人の子供たちが友達になれる日が来るだろうと述べました。

　この、ごく短い演説が、全世界から大変な反響を引き起こしました。公民権が問題になっている時期で、彼、マーティン・ルーサー・キング・ジュニア牧師は、「Five score

1963年8月28日にワシントンD.C.で行われた人種差別撤廃のためのデモ（ワシントン大行進）の際、キング牧師は、リンカン記念館の前で「I Have a Dream（私には夢がある）」という演説をした（写真）。人種差別の撤廃を理想として掲げたこの演説は公民権運動の盛り上がりに大きな影響を与え、その内容はアメリカ国内のみならず世界的に高く評価された。

Dr. King delivered his "I Have a Dream" speech (left) in Washington, D.C., in front of the Lincoln Memorial on August 28, 1963, during a demonstration to abolish racial discrimination (the March on Washington). In the speech, King spoke of his ideal to abolish racial discrimination, and this speech helped to accelerate the Civil Rights Movement. The contents are still evaluated as excellent not only in the U.S., but also around the world.

Martin Luther King, Jr. said, "Five score years ago," which means about 100 years ago, there was Lincoln and he emancipated the black people from the south part of the United States of America. But after five score years, one score means 20 years, so 100 years later, there were still no rights for black people. Even one black lady who was sitting in the bus could not protect her right to sit in the bus with white people. So, his event and his speech was a turning point of the United States of America and the world.

I think this trend comes from famous Lincoln, and of course, Dr. King and Kennedy. And maybe in

years ago」、つまり１００年前に「リンカンがいて、アメリカの南部から黒人を解放した」と述べました。しかし、それから１００年が経っても、黒人には権利がありませんでした。バスに座っていた黒人女性が白人と一緒に座る権利さえ、護(まも)ることができなかったのです。ですから、彼のイベントやスピーチが、アメリカ合衆国および世界にとって"転換点"となったわけです。

"この流れ"は、有名なリンカンや、もちろんキング牧師、そしてケネディに始まったものであると思います。その延

キング牧師の「I Have a Dream（私には夢がある）」演説に先立ち、同じ1963年8月28日にワシントンD.C.で、人種差別撤廃のためのデモ「ワシントン大行進」が行われ、20万人以上が参加した（写真）。
A March on Washington (left) was held on August 28, 1963, in Washington, D.C., advocating the abolishment of racial discrimination. It was held prior to King's "I Have a Dream" speech, with more than 200,000 in attendance.

the extension of this trend, there is Barack Obama, the famous black president. So, we must check this trend, if it's coming from God, if there is any other problem, or if this trend will mean something more from now on, and if there is any American dream in the near future. And I want to know about how and what Dr. King is thinking now.

This is good news for the American people. In America, people are struggling about the next presidency regarding Donald Trump and Hillary Clinton. So, this lecture or this spiritual interview will be helpful to the American people in choosing the next president.

So, then, let's try. Is it OK? All right.

Yuta Okawa Yes.

Ryuho Okawa Then, I will summon Dr. Martin Luther King, Jr. I would like to invite you. Dr. Martin Luther King, Jr., Dr. Martin Luther King, Jr., would you come down here? Would you come down here?

1　キング牧師、自らの運命を語る

長線上に、有名な黒人大統領であるバラク・オバマ氏がいると思われます。ですから、"この流れ"が神から来ているものなのか、ほかに何か課題はあるか、今後、"この流れ"がさらなる意味を持つようになるのか、近い将来、何かアメリカン・ドリームがあるのかについて、チェックしておく必要があります。キング牧師が現在、何をどう考えているのかについても知りたいと思います。

　これはアメリカ人にとっては、福音であると思います。アメリカでは、国民がドナルド・トランプとヒラリー・クリントンをめぐって、次の大統領選に関して争っていますので、この講義あるいは霊言は、米国民が次の大統領を選ぶのに役に立つかと思います。

　では、始めましょう。よろしいですか。はい。

大川裕太　はい。

大川隆法　それでは、マーティン・ルーサー・キング・ジュニア牧師の霊をお呼びいたします。マーティン・ルーサー・キング・ジュニア牧師、マーティン・ルーサー・キング・ジュニア牧師、あなたをお招きいたします。どうかここに降り

Would you accept our interview? Dr. King, would you come down…here?

Martin Luther King, Jr. Agh… Agh… Agh…

Ichikawa Dr. Martin Luther King, Jr.?

King Yes.

Ichikawa Good morning.

King Good morning.

Ichikawa Thank you for your spiritual advent to Happy Science today.

King Happy Science?

Ichikawa Yes.

たまいて、われらのインタビューを受けたまえ。キング牧師、どうか、ここに……降りたまえ。

キング牧師　ああ……ああ……ああ……。

市川　マーティン・ルーサー・キング・ジュニア牧師でいらっしゃいますか。

キング牧師　そうです。

市川　おはようございます。

キング牧師　おはようございます。

市川　本日は、幸福の科学にご降臨くださり、ありがとうございます。

キング牧師　幸福の科学？

市川　はい。

King Ah, famous, famous.

Ichikawa Thank you very much.

King In America, of course.

Ichikawa Thank you very much. It's our pleasure.

Yuta Okawa Thank you.

Guided by God's order and God's love

Ichikawa Today, we would like to ask several questions especially regarding America and its problems and dreams.

First, I would like to ask about your movement, during your age from the 1950s to 1960s. You devoted your life to fight against discrimination, especially to free black people in the United States. So, what made you devote your life to this great movement?

1　キング牧師、自らの運命を語る

キング牧師 ああ、有名ですよ、有名です。

市川 ありがとうございます。

キング牧師 アメリカでも、当然。

市川 ありがとうございます。光栄です。

大川裕太 ありがとうございます。

「神の命(めい)」と「神の愛」に導かれて

市川 本日は、いくつかお伺(うかが)いできればと思います。特にアメリカと、アメリカの課題や夢についてです。

　まず、1950年代から60年代当時の、あなたの運動についてお伺いします。あなたは差別との戦いにご自分の人生を捧げられました。特に、アメリカの黒人に自由をもたらすための戦いです。この偉大な運動に、あなたが人生を捧げる原動力となったものは、何だったのでしょうか。

1 Martin Luther King, Jr. Talks About His Destiny

King Uh-huh.

Ichikawa What was your determination?

King It was destiny, I think so. I'm not the first runner. The latest runner, I think. "Men are created equal," it's written in the Declaration of Independence. But in reality, we were not equal at the time. Even though the famous Abraham Lincoln made a declaration of emancipation for black people*, we were not equal at the time. So, this was my fate and this was my destiny. But it's not something to be respected for. Someone had to do it even if I weren't there. I am not a single human. I am the inspiration from God, itself. So, this was the order from God. I think so.

Ichikawa In your age, you held the policy of nonviolence.

---

* A declaration (executive order) made in 1862 and 1863, during the American Civil War, by then-President Abraham Lincoln. It emancipated the slaves in the Southern Confederate States. The declaration served as the cause behind the movement to free black slaves in America.

1 キング牧師、自らの運命を語る

キング牧師 ああ、うん。

市川 あなたの決意とは、どのようなものだったのでしょうか。

キング牧師 「運命」、ですかね。私は第一走者ではなく、最終走者だったんでしょう。アメリカ独立宣言には「人は平等に創られている」と書いてありますが、現実は、当時、私たちは平等ではありませんでした。有名なアブラハム・リンカンが黒人のために奴隷解放宣言（注）を出しましたが、それでも平等ではなかった。だから、「私の定め」であり、「運命」だったんです。ただ、別に尊敬されるほどのことではありませんよ。私がいなくても、誰かが同じことをしなければならなかったんです。私は一個の人間ではなく、神からのインスピレーションそのものなのです。ですから、「神の命」であったのだろうと思います。

市川 当時は、「非暴力」の方針を貫いていらっしゃいました。

（注）アメリカが南北戦争中の1862年と1863年に、当時の大統領アブラハム・リンカンによって出された、南部連合の奴隷たちの解放を命じた宣言。アメリカで奴隷解放運動が盛んになるきっかけとなった。

1 Martin Luther King, Jr. Talks About His Destiny

King Nonviolence, yeah. Uh-huh.

Ichikawa Why did you choose nonviolence as a policy in your life?

King Hmm…[*folds his arms*]. From the bottom of my heart, I hoped that men are created equal and loved by God equally. In the time of this situation, we had to eliminate hatred from our movement. We needed civil rights. That's true. But it didn't mean we could kill white people who were discriminating us at the time; it didn't mean the life value of white people was lower than black people. God loves all people equally, so I hesitated to demonstrate violence.

Violence only invites violence. Instead of violence, we must have love in our minds and in our hearts. If we can love white people who persecuted us and even the white people who killed us or were violent toward us, we can forgive them from the viewpoint of

1　キング牧師、自らの運命を語る

キング牧師　非暴力、そうです、はい。

市川　なぜ、生涯の方針として非暴力を選ばれたのでしょうか。

キング牧師　うん……（腕組みをする）。私は心の底から、人は神によって平等に創られており、神から等（ひと）しく愛されているものであってほしいと願っていたのです。当時、あの状況では、われわれの運動から憎しみを排除（はいじょ）しなければなりませんでした。公民権を必要としていたのは、その通りです。しかし、だからといって、当時私たちを差別していた白人を殺していいことにはならないですし、白人の命の値打ちが黒人より低いことにもなりません。神がすべての人を等しく愛しておられるがゆえに、私は暴力を示威（じい）することを良しとしなかったのです。

　暴力は暴力を招くだけです。暴力ではなく、心に、この胸に「愛」を持たねばなりません。私たちを迫害し、殺し、私たちに暴力を振るった白人さえも愛することができるのであれば、神の立場に立って彼らを許すことができるでしょう。それこそが「新たな夢」です。それが「新たな世

God. That is the new dream. That is the new world, I think. America must be built on one idea: the idea of equality, the idea of chance, the idea of new creation. So, I hate violence.

2 Faith, Courage and Justice

Yuta Okawa Thank you for coming today, Dr. Martin Luther King.

King Uh-huh [*unfolds his arms and puts his hands together*].

Yuta Okawa I want to ask you about faith. Actually, there were a lot of black activists against the government's policy. For example, there were many predecessors before you like Rosa Parks. She was the one main activist of the bus boycott movement and before her there was Marcus Garvey, who wanted to bring black people back to the African continent. But I think the difference between you and those

界」であると思います。アメリカは、一つの理念の上に建てられねばなりません。「平等」という理念です。「チャンス」という理念、「新たなる創造」という理念です。ですから私は暴力が嫌いなのです。

2　信仰、勇気そして正義

大川裕太　キング牧師、本日はご降臨くださり、ありがとうございます。

キング牧師　はい（腕組みをほどき、両手を組んで聞く）。

大川裕太　私からは、「信仰」についてお伺いしたいと思います。実際は、政府の政策に反対する黒人活動家は大勢いましたし、あなたに先行する活動家も大勢いました。例えばローザ・パークスです。彼女はバス・ボイコット運動の中心的な活動家の一人でした。彼女以前にも、黒人をアフリカ大陸に帰そうとしたマーカス・ガーベイがいました。しかし、あなたとそうした人たちとの違いは「信仰」だと思います。そこで、キリスト教信仰についてお尋ねします。

people lies in faith. So, I'd like to ask you about faith in Christianity. What do you think about your faith and about the importance of it in your life or in your activity?

The power of Jesus' Father that is here now

King Faith is my armor. In some meaning, a spiritual weapon which protects me and which can be used as an aggressive weapon to white people who were persecuting us.

So, without faith, we can do nothing. With faith, if we say, "Move this mountain into the sea," it will be reality. We can. Yes, we can. I moved the mountain into the sea through my faith. Jesus said 2,000 years ago about this Truth. And he was true and he is true. Yeah. We had mountains and mountains of high barrier between black and white. But we destroyed this great barrier and threw it down into the Caribbean Sea. Yes, we could do that. Jesus was right and I believed

2 信仰、勇気そして正義

ご自分の信仰や、ご自分の人生や活動における信仰の大切さについては、どうお考えでいらっしゃいますか。

今も世にある「イエスの父」の力

キング牧師 私にとって信仰は「鎧（よろい）」です。ある意味では、防御（ぼうぎょ）のための霊的な武器でもあり、そしてまた、迫害してくる白人に対して用いることのできる"攻撃用の武器"でもあります。

　信仰なくしては、何事も成（な）しえません。信仰があれば、「この山動きて海に入（い）れ」と言えば、それが現実となります。できます。そう、できるのです。私は信仰により、山を動かして海に入れたのです。イエスは２千年前、この真理を説かれました。彼の言葉は真理でしたし、今も真理です。そう。黒人と白人との間には、山また山の如（ごと）く、高い障壁（しょうへき）がそびえ立っていましたが、われわれはその障壁を打ち砕き、カリブ海へと投げ込んだのです。そう、それができたのです。イエスのおっしゃる通りでした。 私も彼を信じ

in him. So his words were right and are right and will be right. So, faith is everything. Our activity follows our faith.

So, make your faith strong. Make your belief strong in the Truth, in Jesus' words, and the power which came from Heaven through Jesus. It's his Father. The Father's power came through Jesus Christ. It was in this world 2,000 years ago and 50 years ago, and it is now! [*Nods his head many times.*]

Yuta Okawa Thank you very much.

Masashi Ishikawa Thank you, Dr. Martin Luther King. Across the world now and even in America, the number of nonbelievers and atheists are increasing. For example, President Obama said in his first inaugural address, "We are a nation of Christians and Muslims, Jews and Hindus, and nonbelievers." So, even in America, the number of nonbelievers is increasing. How can we try to prevent this trend?

ました。そのお言葉はかつても正しく、今も正しく、これから先も正しいのです。信仰がすべてであり、活動は信仰にあとから付いてくるものです。

　ですから、信仰を強めてください。真理を信じ、イエスの言葉を信じ、イエスを通して天から臨(のぞ)んだ力を信じる心を強めてください。その力とは、「父」です。イエス・キリストを通して「父」の力が臨んでいたのです。それは２千年前もこの世にあり、５０年前にもあり、そして今もあるのです！（何度もうなずく）

大川裕太　ありがとうございます。

石川雅士　キング牧師、ありがとうございます。現在、世界全体で、アメリカにおいてさえ、無宗教の人々、無神論者の数が増加しています。例えば、オバマ大統領は一度目の就任演説の中で、「われわれはキリスト教徒、イスラム教徒、ユダヤ教徒、ヒンズー教徒、そして無宗教者の国です」と言っており、アメリカでさえ無宗教の人の数が増えてきています。どうすればこうした傾向を防ぐことができますでしょうか。

King Oh, why do you need to prevent that trend?

Ishikawa I think you taught us the importance of faith...

King Yeah, yeah.

Ishikawa So, the increasing number of...

King God loves every believer of every religion. Even the nonbelievers are loved by God. God is just waiting for their chance to wake up. So, all men and women are invited to God's party. I think so. No problem. It's just that priests and pastors, or we, religious people, need more power. That's the problem. We lack such kind of aspiration, inspiration and perspiration. So, we must think, "We shouldn't condemn those kind of people." Instead of that, we must do our best. OK?

キング牧師　ほう、なぜ、そうした傾向を防ぐ必要があるんですか。

石川　信仰の大切さを教えていただいたと思いますので……。

キング牧師　はい、そうですよ。

石川　ですから、人数が増えるのは……。

キング牧師　神は、どんな宗教を信じる人も、すべて愛しておられます。無宗教の人でさえ、神に愛されています。神は、ただ、彼らが目覚める機会を待っておられるんです。ですから、すべての男女は神のパーティーに招待されているはずですので、問題ありません。ただ、司祭や牧師など、私たち宗教者に、もっと力が要るというだけのことですよ。問題はそこです。そのためのアスピレーション（熱意）もインスピレーション（霊感）も、パースピレーション（努力）も足りないんです。そういう人を責めるべきではないと思わなければいけません。むしろ、私たちのほうこそ全

King heard the voice of God that is beyond human justice

Yuta Okawa Thank you. Next, I'd like to ask you about your courage.

King College?

Yuta Okawa Courage. You are very courageous.

King You mean braveness?

Yuta Okawa Not a university. Yes, braveness.

King Braveness. OK.

Yuta Okawa Actually, I read in your writings that

力を尽くさなければなりません。よろしいですか。

人間的正義を超える「神の声」を聞いた

大川裕太　ありがとうございます。次に、あなたの「勇気」についてお伺いしたいのですが。

キング牧師　College（大学）？

大川裕太　勇気（courage）です。あなたは勇気に溢れた方ですので。

キング牧師　Braveness（勇気）のことですか。

大川裕太　大学ではなくて。はい、勇気です。

キング牧師　勇気ですね。はい。

大川裕太　お書きになったもので読んだのですが、あなた

you were arrested several times, put in prison a lot of times, and also your home was bombed several times. Around you, there were a lot of enemies and you loved your family, but your family members were also affected by the bombing and you were also nearly killed by one extremist. So, I think you experienced a lot of severe times, but you finally succeeded in your mission. And you didn't quit your activity. What was the source of your courage?

King Aha! There were a lot of prisoners in my time. So, it wasn't so extraordinary, it was common. Black people who were activists usually were thrown in prison, and I was one of them. So, I wasn't an exception.

I think this is a problem of justice. People who are living in America are apt to think that justice is made by law. This means it is made by people who are selected to vote in the United States Congress. And when more than half of the people assist the law, it

2　信仰、勇気そして正義

は何度も逮捕され、投獄されました。また、ご自宅が何度も爆弾の被害に遭いました。周りは敵だらけで、大切なご家族も爆弾の被害に遭われましたし、あなたは過激派の人物に殺されかけました。多くの厳しい時期がありながらも、最終的には使命を果たされ、活動をやめることはありませんでした。その勇気の源泉は何だったのでしょうか。

キング牧師　ああ、はい。囚人は当時たくさんいましたので、特別なことではなく普通だったんですよ。活動家の黒人は、たいてい刑務所に入れられましてね。私もその一人であって、例外ではありませんでした。

　ここは「正義の問題」になってくると思います。アメリカに住んでいる人たちは、「正義は法律によって決まる」と思いがちです。要するに、選ばれた人たちが合衆国議会で投票して決めるものであって、半数以上の人々が支持すれば効力が生じる。それが普通に正義なのだと思いがちです。

becomes effective. They are apt to think that this is the usual justice.

But of course, I know as a religious leader that there is true justice beyond the congress-made justice or the human justice, I mean there is God's justice beyond human justice. I believed in this Truth, so it strengthened me more and more.

The congress established a lot of laws but we, black people, didn't think it was correct or righteous, or in tune with God's justice. So we, believers, could only rely on God's will. We were reading the Bible every day and at that time, we received several inspirations every day, every morning, and every evening.

I've heard God speak, "This law is not good." For example, "This law in Alabama is not good. Black people have the right to ride on the same bus as white people. Or black people and the children of black people have the right to attend the same school as white people and white children." It's true. It can't be bent easily. God's Truth cannot be bent easily. It is a

2 信仰、勇気そして正義

　しかし、私は宗教的リーダーとして、当然、議会が決めた正義や人間の正義を超える「真の正義」があることを知っています。人間的正義を超える「神の正義」です。私はこの真理を信じていたので、さらにさらに強くなることができました。

　議会はいろいろな法律を制定しましたが、われわれ黒人はそれが正しいとも、神の正義に適（かな）っているとも思えませんでした。われわれ信仰者が頼れるものは、神のご意志以外に、なかったのです。私たちは毎日『聖書』を読んで、日々、毎朝、毎晩、インスピレーションを受けていました。

　私には、神が「この法律は良くない」とおっしゃるのが聞こえたのです。例えば、「アラバマ州のこの法律は良くない。黒人には白人と同じバスに乗る権利がある。あるいは、黒人や黒人の子供には、白人や白人の子供と同じ学校に通う権利がある」と。それが真実であり、みだりに曲げることはできません。神の真理は、みだりに曲げることはできません。直（なお）きものです。変えられるものではないの

straight one. It cannot be changed. God said that.

[*Puts his hands beside his head imagining God's voice and closes his eyes.*] I've heard the voice of God. God ordered me, "Emancipate black children. They have equal rights like white children. They both are the new hopes of America."

Ichikawa Thank you. As you mentioned justice, I would like to ask about justice. In the modern age, Islamic nations have their own justice based on the Qur'an, justice for Allah. Or in Christian countries, they have their own justice, God's justice. In this world, there are many kinds of justice. So, there are now many conflicts among nations. How do we overcome these conflicts, like holding the true justice as you said?

King Conflicts are just among people. God does not cause conflicts. If Allah of Islamic people is the same God as we think He is, then Allah is the God of love,

です。神は、そう言われました。

　(神の声をイメージするかのように、両手を耳のそばにかざし、目を閉じて) 私は神の声を聞いたのです。神は私にお命じになりました。「黒人の子らを解放せよ。彼らには、白人の子らと同じ権利がある。彼らは共に、アメリカの新しい希望なのだ」と。

市川　ありがとうございます。正義の話が出ましたので、正義についてさらに伺いたいと思います。現代では、イスラム教国においては、コーランに基づく独自の正義、アッラーのための正義があります。また、キリスト教国においても、彼ら独自の正義、神の正義があります。世界に数多くの正義があり、そのため、国家間で多くの紛争が起きています。どうすれば、こうした紛争を乗り越え、あなたがおっしゃるように本当の正義を掲げることができるのでしょうか。

キング牧師　紛争は、人間同士の間にのみ、あるものです。神は紛争を起こされません。イスラム教徒のアッラーが、私たちが考えるのと同じ神であるのなら、アッラーは愛の

Allah is the God of mercy, Allah is with weak people, Allah is with black people and Allah is with Islamic people. No problem.

So, transparency of the true belief is very important. People are apt to think of the Truth for their own benefit. It's a problem. Truth is not a benefit. Truth itself is very valuable. We are not living only by bread. We are living by the Truth. If people accept what I say today, even the Islamic people and black people can both believe each other, trust each other and believe in one God, I think.

3 Slavery, Discrimination and War

Yuta Okawa Thank you very much. Next, I'd like to ask you about the problems at church in the United States.

King Problems at church?

神であり、アッラーは慈悲の神であり、アッラーは弱き者と共にあり、アッラーは黒人と共にあり、イスラム教徒と共にあります。何も問題はありません。

　ですから、本物の信仰が持つ透明さが、きわめて大事です。人は、真理を自分の都合(つごう)のいいように考えがちです。問題はそこです。真理は利益ではありません。真理はそれ自体で、きわめて尊いものなのです。人は、パンのみによって生きているのではありません。真理によって生きているのです。今日の私の話を受け入れていただければ、イスラム教徒であっても黒人であっても、互いに信じ合い、信頼し合い、一つの神を信じることができると思います。

3　奴隷制度、人種差別、戦争

大川裕太　ありがとうございます。次に、アメリカの教会の問題についてお伺いしたいと思います。

キング牧師　教会の問題ですか。

Yuta Okawa Yes. As you mentioned in your preaching, America is a class society and sometimes churches help this situation. For example, in some cases, white people go to white people's churches only and black people go to black people's churches only, and sometimes, your activity was not supported by white churches. You were very disappointed at this situation and even now, such situation is still continuing in the United States. What do you think about Americans' class society and churches?

White people have not reflected upon their history of slavery

King It's a very deep and difficult question. About 400 years ago, we were slaves. At the time, we were slaves from the African continent, as you know. We were working for cotton farmers, and we were of course slaves, so we didn't have civil power or rights. We were robots, machine-like people or humanoids.

大川裕太　はい。あなたが説教の中で指摘されたように、アメリカは階級社会であり、しばしば教会がその状況に手を貸している場合もあります。例えば、白人は白人の教会にしか行かず、黒人は黒人の教会にしか行かないことがあります。あなたの活動は白人の教会の支持を得られないこともあり、あなたは非常に落胆されました。今もなおアメリカでは、そうした状況が続いています。アメリカの階級社会と教会については、どう思われますか。

白人は奴隷制度についての反省ができていない

キング牧師　それは実に根深い、難しい質問です。４００年ほど前は、われわれは奴隷でした。ご存じの通り、アフリカ大陸から来た奴隷です。綿花を栽培する農家のために働いて、奴隷ですから当然、市民権もなかったし、「ロボット」か、「機械並みに扱われる人間」か、「ヒト型ロボット」みたいなものでした。

But we are human. This is a radical thinking. Even the people, I mean the priests from Roman Catholic, for example, the Jesuits or those who came from Spain or Portugal, discriminated the black people in the African continent. They looked down upon us as apes. Do you understand the word *ape*? Some kind of black monkey.

So, we were sold to the United States and became slaves like the Jewish or the Israelis who were sold to Egypt more than 3,000 years ago. Jewish people had been slaves in the great empire of Egypt for about 400 years at the time of the emancipation by Moses, the Exodus. At that time, they found the Land of Canaan. It's the same as how our Pilgrim Fathers found the continent of America. So, slavery was a bad custom of people or humankind.

Even now, the white people in the world cannot reflect upon themselves that slavery was a bad thing which is very far from the heart of God, I think. But my work has fallen short of that point, so the next

3 奴隷制度、人種差別、戦争

しかし、われわれも人間なのです。これは革命的な考え方です。ローマ・カトリックの聖職者や、イエズス会や、スペインやポルトガルから来ていた人たちでさえ、アフリカ大陸で黒人を差別していました。彼らは、われわれを類人猿であるかのように見下していました。「類人猿」というのはお分かりですか。黒い猿の一種ですよ。

私たちはアメリカに売られて、ユダヤ人の如く奴隷にされました。3千年以上前、エジプトに売られたイスラエルの民です。モーセが出エジプトで奴隷を解放した時は、ユダヤ人はエジプトの大帝国で400年間、奴隷だったのです。そこから彼らはカナンの地を見出しました。アメリカ大陸を見出したピルグリム・ファーザーズと同じです。ですから奴隷制度は、人類の悪しき慣習だったのです。

いまだに世界の白人たちは、奴隷制度が神の心からかけ離れた悪しきものであったという反省が、できていないと思われます。ただ、私の仕事はその点で及びませんでしたので、次に来る人々、選ばれし人々が、この仕事を完遂せ

people, the next selected people must accomplish this work. Eliminating discrimination against the colored people is required from God.

Yuta Okawa Thank you very much.

The next American president must apologize to Japan about the atomic bombings

Ishikawa I would like to ask you more about that. When the League of Nations was established, Japan put forth the racial equality proposal*...

King Racial equality proposal, OK.

Ishikawa ...Yes, to eliminate racial discrimination. The proposal was rejected by America and the UK, but

---

* A proposal submitted by Japan in 1919, after World War I, to the League of Nations Commission at the Paris Peace Conference, demanding that racial equality be included in the League of Nations Charter. The proposal was denied due to strong oppositions by countries such as the U.S., Australia and Britain. Japan was the first to clearly state the abolishment of racial discrimination at an international conference.

ねばなりません。有色人種に対する差別を撤廃することが、神の求めておられることなのです。

大川裕太　ありがとうございます。

次の米大統領は日本に原爆投下を謝罪すべき

石川　それについて、さらにお伺いしたいと思います。国際連盟が設立されたとき、日本は「人種的差別撤廃提案」（注）を提出しました。

キング牧師　「人種的差別撤廃提案」、はい。

石川　はい、人種差別を撤廃するためです。その提案はアメリカとイギリスによって否決されましたが、公民権運動

（注）第一次世界大戦後の1919年に、パリ講和会議・国際連盟委員会において日本が提出した、人種差別撤廃を国際連盟規約に明記するべきとの提案。アメリカやオーストラリア、イギリス等の強硬な反対で否決された。国際会議の場で人種差別撤廃を明確に主張したのは日本が世界で初めてだった。

NAACP (National Association for the Advancement of Colored People)*, maybe the core organization of Civil Rights Movement, supported Japan's proposal. So, in a sense, I think Japan's movement before World War II and the Civil Rights Movement are interconnected. What are your thoughts on that?

King Uh…Ah…

Ishikawa The rise of Japan or the rise of Asian countries.

King It's a good thing. It is regarding the yellow people. Yellow people are also discriminated by white people. That was the reason behind the Pacific War between the United States and Japan. If Japanese people were white people, the atomic bombs would not have been

---

* One of the oldest civil rights organization in the U.S. and a leader group in the movement to free black slaves. The group offered comments of gratitude when Japan submitted the Racial Equality Proposal to the League of Nations Commission.

の核となった組織とも言えるＮＡＡＣＰ（全米黒人地位向上協会。注）は日本の提案を支持しました。ですから、ある意味で、「第二次大戦前の日本の運動」と「公民権運動」はつながっていると思います。そこについては、どうお考えですか。

キング牧師　うーん、ああ……。

石川　日本の台頭(たいとう)やアジアの国々の台頭です。

キング牧師　いいことでした。黄色人種に関することですね。黄色人種も白人に差別されています。それが日米間の太平洋戦争の理由でしたし、日本人が白人だったら原爆投下はなかったでしょう。アメリカ大統領はドイツに原爆を落とすことはできませんでしたが、広島と長崎には落とし

（注）アメリカで最も古い公民権運動組織の一つで、黒人解放運動における指導的な組織。日本が国際連盟委員会において「人種的差別撤廃提案」を提案した際には、日本に対して感謝のコメントを発表した。

dropped, I think. American president couldn't drop it on Germany, but American president dropped it onto Hiroshima and Nagasaki. It's a shameful fact of the American people.

Mr. Obama recently went to Hiroshima and prayed for the dead, but he did not apologize to the families of the deceased. It's not enough. He, I mean Mr. Barack Obama, should apologize to them in place of former President Truman. It's a bad thing. Gods don't like that kind of massacre. It's the same as the German

3 奴隷制度、人種差別、戦争

ました。これはアメリカ人にとって恥ずべき事実です。

　オバマ氏は最近、広島に行って亡くなった人々のために祈りましたが、遺族に謝罪はしなかった。これは不十分です。彼は、つまりバラク・オバマ氏は、トルーマン元大統領に代わって謝るべきです。悪いことをしたんですから。神々はそのような大虐殺(だいぎゃくさつ)を好まれません。ドイツがユダヤ人を虐殺した、アウシュビッツの出来事と同じです。どち

2016年5月27日、バラク・オバマ大統領は、現職のアメリカ合衆国大統領としては初めて、第二次世界大戦の際に原爆を投下された広島を訪問した。同氏は安倍晋三首相とともに広島平和記念公園、広島平和記念資料館を訪れ、原爆死没者慰霊碑に献花した後、「核兵器なき世界」に向けた演説をした（写真）。
On May 27, 2016, President Barack Obama visited Hiroshima, the site of the atomic bomb dropping in World War II, as the first U.S. president to do so while in office. After visiting the Hiroshima Peace Memorial Park and the Hiroshima Peace Memorial Museum with Prime Minister Abe, and offering flowers at the Memorial Cenotaph, President Obama made a speech, calling for "a world without nuclear weapons" (left).

massacre of Jewish people, the event of Auschwitz. These are crimes against humankind. So, the next American president must say, "We are sorry," to the Japanese people. This is the beginning of abolishing atomic bombs from the world. I think so.

Vietnam War, Gulf War, and Iraq War

Ishikawa Thank you so much. Now, American justice is shaken and wavering. And I think you spoke out against the Vietnam War.

King Oh, yeah.

Ishikawa Recently, we had the Iraq War, and former President Bush led American nations and British people to the Iraq War. And this war is now severely criticized. Could you tell us about your view on war and peace?

らも人類に対する犯罪です。ですから次のアメリカ大統領は、日本人に「申し訳ありません」と謝らなければなりません。それが、世界から原爆を捨て去る始まりであると思います。

ベトナム戦争、湾岸戦争、イラク戦争

石川　ありがとうございます。今、アメリカの正義は揺さぶられ、揺らいでいます。あなたはベトナム戦争に反対されていたと思います。

キング牧師　ああ、そうでした。

石川　最近では、イラク戦争がありました。ブッシュ前大統領は米国民とイギリス国民をイラク戦争に引きずり込みました。この戦争は現在では厳しい批判にさらされています。戦争と平和についてのお考えをお聞かせいただけますでしょうか。

3 Slavery, Discrimination and War

King [*Folds his arms again.*] My view on war and peace.

Ishikawa Yes.

King The Vietnam War was bad. It was an American invasion. I think so. It's a crime. They, the American people in my time, killed maybe millions of North and South Vietnamese people and also more than 50,000 American young soldiers were killed in that land. This is a tragedy, I think.

I also know about the recent Iraq War. About ten years before that, there was the Gulf War. President George H. Bush led this. And 10 years later, the son, President Bush led the Iraq War. I can understand the reason why. At the World Trade Center, about 3,000 American people were killed. It's almost the same as the death toll in Hawaii, Honolulu from the first attack of the Japanese army in 1941, including those who died on the battleship, Arizona. So, Bush Jr. wanted to take

3 奴隷制度、人種差別、戦争

キング牧師 （再び腕組みをする）戦争と平和についての考えですね。

石川 はい。

キング牧師 ベトナム戦争は「悪」でした。アメリカによる「侵略」だったと思います。「犯罪」です。当時アメリカ人は、おそらく何百万人もの南北ベトナム人を殺害し、若きアメリカ兵も５万人以上、かの地で死にました。悲劇だと思います。

　近年のイラク戦争のことも知っていますよ。その１０年ほど前には湾岸戦争がありました。父ブッシュ大統領がやりました。そして１０年後に、息子の方のブッシュ大統領がイラク戦争をやりました。その理由は分かります。ワールドトレードセンターで約３千人のアメリカ人が殺されました。これは、1941年に日本軍がハワイのホノルルを最初に攻撃した時の、戦艦アリゾナ号の死者数も含めた死者数とほぼ同じです。だから息子ブッシュはその"仕返し"がしたかったんでしょう。それは分かります。

revenge about that. I can understand.

But they killed hundreds of thousands of people in Iraq and in the end, Saddam Hussein, the president of Iraq, was hanged. It's not legal, I think. If there were conflicts or wars between two countries, the victorious country can hang the other country's prime minister or president. This is just revenge, not vengeance. It must depend on the world fairness. It's just revenge, so it's not good. I think so.

These two or three wars were not required from God. They were American justice, I know. But American justice didn't come from God. American justice came from the anger of the American people. I think so.

Ishikawa Additionally, some people say that the Iraq War was not correct because they couldn't get approval from the United Nations. For example, the Gulf War was supported by China and Russia. So, how about the justice of the United Nations?

しかし、彼らはイラク人を何十万人も殺し、最終的にはサダム・フセイン大統領は絞首刑(こうしゅけい)にされました。あれは合法的ではないと思います。二国間で紛争ないし戦争があって、勝った国が相手国のトップ、つまり首相や大統領を処刑していいというのは、単なる"仕返し"であって、「正当な報復」ではありません。世界から見た公平性に基づかなければいけません。単なる"仕返し"であり、よくないことだと思います。

　これら二つないし三つの戦争は、神の求めによるものではありませんでした。「アメリカの正義」であったことは分かりますが、アメリカの正義は神から来たものではなかった。アメリカの正義は、アメリカ国民の怒りによるものだったと思います。

石川　それに加えて、「国連の承認を得られなかったのだからイラク戦争は正しくない」と言う人もいます。例えば、湾岸戦争は中国とロシアの支持を得ていました。国連の正義については、いかがでしょうか。

King I don't know exactly. But a war which massacres tens of thousands of people, or more than that, cannot be believed to be done in the name of God. Sometimes we must legally kill the criminals who killed a lot of people. In some meaning, we must hesitatingly support such kind of deed by our nation. But a battle that kills more than tens of thousands of people is not so good.

Even during Lincoln's presidency, more than 600,000 people were killed in the Civil War of the United States of America. America was on the verge of separation between the North and the South; a unified America or a separated America. That was the choice at that time. I respect Lincoln, and before the Civil War, they must have talked a lot through our congress and made the decision, so I cannot blame Abraham Lincoln. He's a great person and my predecessor, so I cannot say exactly, but a war which kills more than tens of thousands of people is not justified.

3 奴隷制度、人種差別、戦争

キング牧師 詳しくは分かりませんが、数万人あるいはそれ以上の人数を大量虐殺するような戦争は、神の名のもとに行われたとは思えませんね。人を大勢殺した犯罪者を合法的に死刑にしなければいけないこともあります。ある意味、国家によるそうした行為は、やむを得ず支持しなくてはなりませんが、数万人以上もの人が戦場で死ぬのは、いいことではありません。

リンカンが大統領の時にも、アメリカ合衆国の南北戦争で６０万人以上の人が死にましたが、あれはアメリカが南北に分裂するかどうかの瀬戸際でした。アメリカの「統一か・分裂か」の選択の時だったのです。私はリンカンを尊敬しておりますし、南北戦争の前には、議会を通じて議論が尽くされ、判断がなされたはずですので、アブラハム・リンカンを責めることはできません。偉大な方であり、私にとっては先駆者ですので、正確な言い方はできませんが、数万人以上も人が死ぬ戦争は、正当化されるものではありません。

4 Solve Poverty and Immigration Issues by Providing Equal Chances

Yuta Okawa Related to the problem of the Vietnam War, I'd like to ask more. Actually, a lot of historical researchers say you changed your opinion after the success of the Civil Rights Movement. After the Civil Rights Movement succeeded and Civil Rights Act was enforced, you started a movement against social injustice like poor people's situation. You started Poor People's March instead of March on Washington and at that time, you mentioned that American people spend a lot of money on war, but spend little money on poor people, so you said this was injustice. And because of this, you were considered as a spy for communists by FBI Director, J. Edgar Hoover. What was your true opinion about social situation or communism or such American situations?

4　貧困と移民問題は「チャンスの平等」で解決を

大川裕太　ベトナム戦争の問題に関連して、もう少しお聞きしたいと思います。「あなたは公民権運動が成功した後、意見を変えた」という歴史研究家が大勢います。公民権運動が成功し、公民権法が施行された後、あなたは貧困という社会的不正義に対して反対し始めました。ワシントン大行進に代わって「貧者の行進」を始め、その際に、「アメリカ国民は戦争に大金を費やしていながら、貧しい人々のためにはあまり金を使わない。これは不正義である」と主張して、そのため、ＦＢＩ長官のＪ・エドガー・フーバーから共産主義のスパイとみなされていました。アメリカが置かれていた社会状況や共産主義について、本心では、どういうご意見だったのでしょうか。

America should be the champion of the countries of chances

King OK, OK. Japan is a beautiful and respectable country. But my country at my time was not so good, I think. One part of the American people were very rich, but all the black people, some white people and the other immigrants were very poor. The poor black people were sent first to Vietnam to kill Asian people, and after that, the white people were sent. The death rate of young black people was very high, and the death rate of the white people was low.

We were also discriminated for social problems. So, we were human, but undergrade human at that time. Civil rights weren't enough. We needed more rights. I just asked for chance — the right for chance, the right to get liberty, the right to get prosperity, or in easy phrase, to get more money. But even such chances were not provided at that time.

So, I'm not, in reality, a communist. We, black

4 貧困と移民問題は「チャンスの平等」で解決を

アメリカはチャンスの国のチャンピオンであれ

キング牧師 はい、分かりました。日本は美しい、尊敬に値(あたい)する国です。しかし、私の頃は、わが国はあまり良くなかったと思いますね。一部のアメリカ人は非常に裕福でも、すべての黒人、一部の白人、その他の移民は非常に貧しかったんですよ。最初に貧しい黒人から、アジア人を殺すためにベトナムに送り込まれて、白人が行くのはそのあとでした。若い黒人の死亡率は非常に高く、白人の死亡率は低かったのです。

　われわれは社会問題においても差別されていました。人間なのに、あの頃は人間以下でした。公民権だけでは不十分です。われわれには、さらなる権利が必要です。私は、とにかく「機会」を求めたんです。「機会に対する権利」です。「自由を手にする権利」、「繁栄を手にする権利」です。簡単に言うと、「もっとお金を稼(かせ)ぐための権利」ですが、当時はそうした機会さえ与えられていなかったのです。
　実際は、私は共産主義者ではありません。われわれ黒人

people, were already poor enough, so I just asked for chance; the rights to try to succeed in business or try to go to school to receive good education. It's a springboard for success. We needed education. We needed transportation. We needed schools. We needed the freedom of activity that produced chance.

America should be the champion of the countries of chances. This is the pride of America. It's not only for white people, but for all the people from the world. America was made up from a lot of colored people or immigrants. This is the American pride. These immigrants who came from a lot of countries have the chance to succeed. This is the American dream, American beauty and American blessing. So, I'm not a communist. I just sought for the chance to get property or to give money to poor people.

Yuta Okawa I guess from your opinion, maybe you think that the American government should resolve the problems of poor people first. So, you mean,

は、すでに十分、貧しかったので、私は、とにかく「チャンスを求めた」のです。ビジネスで成功する権利や、いい教育を受けるために学校に行く権利です。それらが成功への踏み台になるからです。私たちには、教育も必要、交通手段も必要、学校も必要、活動の自由も必要で、それが"チャンス"を生むのです。

　アメリカは、"チャンスの国"のチャンピオンでなければ駄目なんです。それこそがアメリカのプライドなのです。白人のためだけでなく、全世界から来た人々のためです。アメリカは、多くの有色人種や移民から成り立っている国で、それがアメリカのプライドなのです。これら、多くの国から来た移民たちに、「成功のチャンス」がある。それこそがアメリカン・ドリームであり、アメリカの美しさであり、アメリカの祝福なのです。ですから、私は共産主義者ではなく、財産を得る機会や、貧しい人にお金を差し出す機会を求めただけです。

大川裕太　お考えから察するに、「アメリカ政府は、まずは貧しい人々の問題を解決すべきである」というお考えでしょうか。政府が社会的不正義を解決するまでは、アメリ

the United States is not the army of God unless its government resolves social injustice?

King "Social injustice" is a good word, yeah.

Yuta Okawa Thanks. Is that your opinion?

King Huh?

Yuta Okawa Is your opinion, "The United States is not the army of God unless the American government resolves social injustice"?

King You major in international politics, so your thinking is a little different from common people. You are thinking about the world in a strategic meaning. It's a different one. I cannot think from the standpoint of international politics and the strategy of the country.

カは神の軍隊ではないということなのでしょうか。

キング牧師　「社会的不正義」というのは、上手（うま）い言い方ですね。

大川裕太　ありがとうございます。それがあなたのご意見でしょうか。

キング牧師　はい？

大川裕太　「アメリカは、政府が社会的不公平を解決しない限り、神の軍隊ではない」というご意見なのでしょうか。

キング牧師　あなたは国際政治を専攻しているので、普通の人と少し思考が違うんですよ。あなたは世界を戦略的観点から考えていますが、それはまた別のことです。私は、そういった国際政治や国家戦略といった観点から考えることはできません。それは知事や政治家次第です。私は政治

That kind of issue depends on the governor or the politician. I'm not a politician, so I don't know about that. I'm a religious leader, so I'm thinking from the bottom of my heart about the people.

If there is some kind of difference between you and I, it's the difference of viewpoint. I'm thinking about human rights, so in the meaning of human rights, there must be several things that need to be changed before the American army kills other people for world justice. Before that, we must change and realize equality in our nation. Then, that nation will be guided by God and can remake the world and rebuild the world as the country of justice. I think so.

We must change first. Next, we can choose the plan of the world. Traditional American justice is not enough; it's not a complete plan of God, I think. But your strategic mind is above my recognition, so if you want to say something in addition to my opinion, it's your option. You can insist about that.

郵便はがき

```
1 0 7 - 8 7 9 0
```
112

料金受取人払郵便

赤坂局
承認

8228

差出有効期間
平成29年11月
30日まで
(切手不要)

東京都港区赤坂2丁目10−14
幸福の科学出版 (株)
愛読者アンケート係 行

フリガナ お名前		男・女	歳
ご住所　〒　　　　　　　　都道 　　　　　　　　　　　　　府県			
お電話（　　　　　）　−			
e-mail アドレス			
ご職業	①会社員 ②会社役員 ③経営者 ④公務員 ⑤教員・研究者 ⑥自営業 ⑦主婦 ⑧学生 ⑨パート・アルバイト ⑩他（　　　　）		
今後、弊社の新刊案内などをお送りしてもよろしいですか？　（はい・いいえ）			

愛読者プレゼント☆アンケート

『キング牧師 天国からのメッセージ』のご購読ありがとうございました。今後の参考とさせていただきますので、下記の質問にお答えください。抽選で幸福の科学出版の書籍・雑誌をプレゼント致します。
（発表は発送をもってかえさせていただきます）

1 本書をどのようにお知りになりましたか？

①新聞広告を見て [新聞名： 　　　　　　　　　　　　　　　　　　　　　]
②ネット広告を見て [ウェブサイト名： 　　　　　　　　　　　　　　　　]
③書店で見て　　　　④ネット書店で見て　　　　⑤幸福の科学出版のウェブサイト
⑥人に勧められて　　⑦幸福の科学の小冊子　　　⑧月刊「ザ・リバティ」
⑨月刊「アー・ユー・ハッピー？」　　⑩ラジオ番組「天使のモーニングコール」
⑪その他 (　　　　　　　　　　　　　　　　　　　　　　　　　　　　　)

2 本書をお読みになったご感想をお書きください。

3 今後読みたいテーマなどがありましたら、お書きください。

ご感想を匿名にて広告等に掲載させていただくことがございます。ご記入いただきました個人情報については、同意なく他の目的で使用することはございません。
ご協力ありがとうございました。

家ではありませんので、そういうことは分かりません。宗教指導者ですので、心底(しんそこ)、人々のことを考えているんです。

　あなたと、ある種の違いや距離があるとしたら、視点の違いです。私は「人権」について考えていますから、人権という意味においては、米軍が世界正義のために他国の人々を殺す前に、変えねばならないことがいくつかあるはずです。その前に自分たちが変わり、自分たちの国に平等を実現しなければいけません。そういう国であって初めて、神の後押(あとお)しを得て、正義の国として世界を創り直し、世界を再建することができると思います。

　まずは、私たちが変わらなければなりません。世界計画を選ぶことができるのは、その次です。伝統的なアメリカの正義では不十分ですし、神の完璧な計画でもないと思います。ただ、あなたの戦略的思考は私の認識力を超えていますので、私の意見に加えて何かをおっしゃりたいのであれば、それはあなたのご自由であり、主張なさって結構です。

Government should provide equal conditions to the minority

Yuta Okawa No, I understand your position. This year, Master's book, *The Laws of Justice* came out in the United States, and in this book, Master mentioned President Barack Obama's foreign policy. I think his policy is at least good for the American people. For example, the increase of social welfare is very good for American poor people, but he concentrated only about that problem, so foreign policy of the United States is becoming weaker and weaker. Master was worried about that.

4 貧困と移民問題は「チャンスの平等」で解決を

政府は弱者にも「平等な条件」を提供せよ

大川裕太　いえ、私もあなたのお立場は分かります。今年、総裁先生の『正義の法』という著書がアメリカで出版されまして、この本の中で総裁先生は、バラク・オバマ大統領の外交政策について述べていらっしゃいます。彼の政策は「米国民にとってはいい政策」でしょう。例えば社会福祉の増加は、貧しい米国民には非常に有り難いことです。ですが、彼がその問題にばかり集中したので、アメリカの外交政策はどんどん弱くなってきています。総裁先生は、それを心配されたのだと思います。

2016年度法シリーズ『正義の法』（写真左・幸福の科学出版刊）。同書の英訳版『The Laws of Justice』（写真右・New York: IRH Press, 2016）が北米で発刊された。

The 2016 Laws series, *Seigi-no-Ho*, published in Japan (photo left). Its English-translated version, *The Laws of Justice*, was published in North America (photo right).

King But one percent of the nation has the same amount of property as that of the remaining 99 percent; this is the economic status quo. This is the American reality. And if we look at the world, maybe ten percent of the people have the same amount of property as that of the rest of the 90 percent. This is the world reality. So, I understand the difference between two kinds of people, the poor people and the rich people. Rich people depend on their efforts, talents, fate, or good karma from the past life [*laughs*], I don't know exactly, but now there is a lot of poverty in the world.

We can do one thing. If richer people have too much money or enough wealth to feed their families, they can use their money for the poor class people in the United States and in the world. Poverty is a hotbed of crimes. Criminals come from poor areas. For example, Harlem in New York has a lot of poor people and it produces a lot of criminals. We don't have Batman in reality [*laughs*]. If we have Batman, Superman or other heroes, we can settle the problem but we don't. So, we

4　貧困と移民問題は「チャンスの平等」で解決を

キング牧師　ただ、経済の現状は、国民の１パーセントが残り９９パーセントと同じだけの財産を所有していますよね。それがアメリカの現実です。世界を見渡してみても、１０パーセントの人たちが９０パーセントと同じだけの財産を所有しているのかもしれません。それが世界の現実です。二種類の人たちに違いがあることは理解しています。「貧しい人」と「豊かな人」ですね。「豊かな人」は、努力や才能、運命、あるいは過去世の善きカルマかどうか分かりませんが（笑）、それらに頼っているわけですけれども、世界は貧困で溢れています。

　一つ、できることがあります。「豊かな人」にお金が余っていて、家族を十分養える富があるなら、そのお金をアメリカや世界の貧困層のために使うことが可能です。貧困は犯罪の温床です。犯罪は貧しい地区で起きるんですね。例えばニューヨークのハーレムには貧しい人がたくさんいて、犯罪が多発しています。現実世界にはバットマンはいませんので（笑）。バットマンやスーパーマンやその他のヒーローがいれば問題は解決できますが、いませんので、予算を使って平等な条件を整える必要があります。要する

must use our budget and provide equal conditions. I mean the government should use money or budget to give to poor people, including black people, Islamic people, other colored people or poor white people, at least the minimum level of living and the educational chance to get a job. These people are weak and are apt to commit crimes. This must be the basic policy of the government, I think. I'm not a governor, and I'm not a politician, I'm not a statesman, so I cannot say enough, but I hope so.

Black people are also humans with souls and intelligence

Ishikawa Thank you so much. Especially in America, the issue of poverty is related to the issue of immigration.

King Immigration.

に、政府の資金・予算を、黒人やイスラム教徒、有色人種や白人の貧困層などの貧しい人たちに、最低限の生活水準と、仕事に就けるだけの教育の機会を与えるために使うべきです。彼らは弱者で犯罪に走りやすいからです。政府の基本政策はそうあるべきだと思います。私は知事でもないし、政治屋でも政治家でもありませんので、十分には語れませんが、それが望ましいと思いますよ。

黒人も人間であり、魂があり知能がある

石川　ありがとうございます。特にアメリカでは、貧困問題は移民問題と関連があります。

キング牧師　移民ですね。

Ishikawa Yeah. For example, Donald Trump said...

King Ah, I know.

Ishikawa ...that immigration has produced lower wages and higher unemployment. So, that's why he wants to limit the number of immigrants and tries to build "the Great Wall." When Pope Francis visited America last year, he was also against Donald Trump's comment or stance. From the religious perspective, we need to be tolerant, but what do you think about the issue of immigration?

King Hmm...Ah...[*Sighs.*] It depends on the country's policy. America used to have a policy to welcome immigrants because immigrants have a lot of vitality. For example, at the time of the Second World War, a lot of clever Jewish people escaped from Germany, transited through England and into the United States. These people were very dedicated to the American

石川　はい。例えば、ドナルド・トランプは……。

キング牧師　ああ、知ってますよ。

石川　……低賃金や失業率の高さは移民のせいだと言っています。それを理由に、彼は移民の数を制限して"万里の長城"を築こうとしているわけです。フランシスコ法王は昨年アメリカを訪問した際に、ドナルド・トランプの発言や姿勢に反対しました。宗教的観点からは「寛容さ」が必要ですが、移民問題についてはどのようにお考えでしょうか。

キング牧師　うーん。ああ（ため息）、その国の「国策」次第ですね。かつてのアメリカは国策として、移民を歓迎していました。移民には活力がありますのでね。例えば第二次大戦の際には、ユダヤ人で頭のいい人たちが大量に、ドイツからイギリス経由でアメリカに逃げてきました。この人たちは、科学技術や教育の力、思想、学術的進歩などを通して、アメリカの繁栄に多大な貢献を成しました。で

prosperity through their scientific technology, educational power, philosophy or through academic progress. So, America benefited a lot from Jewish immigrants.

We, black people, were misunderstood. We were just used like tractors or Jeep, or in another meaning, horses or ox-like working power. Black people were used only as labor power. White people looked down upon us as if we didn't have enough intelligence because we're not human beings. Roman Catholic priests historically taught: "Black people don't have any soul in them. They are equal to animals." So I, or we, Civil Rights Movement leaders insisted that we, black people also have souls, one soul in one body like white people. This is the point we insisted on. We have souls, so it means we have intelligence. And if we have chance of equal education, we can study and make progress.

For example, I have a college degree. Mr. Barack Obama has a Harvard Law School degree. Even the

すから、アメリカはユダヤ移民によって大いに恩恵を受けたわけです。

　われわれ黒人は誤解されていたんですよ。ただただ、トラクターかジープか、あるいは馬か牛同然の労働力として使われるだけだった。黒人は労働力としてしか使われなかったんです。「人間ではないので知能が足りない」として、白人から見下されていました。ローマ・カトリックの司祭たちが、「黒人には魂がなく、動物と同じである」と歴史的に教えてきたんです。ですから、私たち公民権運動の指導者は、「われわれ黒人にも魂はあるのだ。白人同様、一人ひとりに魂が備わっているのだ」と主張しました。それが、私たちの主張したポイントです。「黒人にも魂がある、つまり知能があるのだ」ということです。「平等な教育の機会があれば、勉強もできるし、進歩もしていけるのだ」ということです。

　例えば、私は大学の学位を取りましたし、バラク・オバマ氏もハーバードのロー・スクールの学位を持っています

ape-like black people can graduate from Harvard. That's the truth. So, we need aids from the rich, white people and it must be the main policy to accommodate colored people who don't have enough conditions to succeed in business. Is this all right or not? Did I misunderstand you?

5 On Sexual Discrimination and Gun Control

Ichikawa Thank you very much for your answer. Now, I'd like to ask about current issues.

King Current issues!? A little difficult for me. OK.

King's stance on the gender issue

Ichikawa There is still racial discrimination in the United States. It's not only toward black people, but

よね。猿のような黒人でもハーバードを卒業できるわけです。それが真実です。ですから、われわれには裕福な白人からの援助が必要であり、それが、ビジネスで成功するための条件に乏(とぼ)しい有色人種を受け入れる際の、主要政策であるべきです。よろしかったでしょうか。ご質問を誤解してしまいましたか。

5　性差別と銃規制について

市川　お答えいただき、まことにありがとうございます。今度は、時事問題についてお伺いしたいと思います。

キング牧師　時事問題ですか。私には、やや難しいんですが、どうぞ。

ジェンダー問題に関するキングの見解

市川　米国には、今も人種差別があります。黒人だけでなく、ヒスパニックやイスラム教徒に対する人種差別ですが、

also toward Hispanic or Islamic people. In addition to that, there is another kind of discrimination: sexual discrimination. In abbreviation, it's called LGBT — lesbian, gay, bisexual and transgender.

King Another difficult problem.

Ichikawa It's another complicated discrimination. How do you see these kinds of discrimination, like racial discrimination and sexual discrimination? Do you have any solution for the future?

King Hmm. My task was racial discrimination, so hmm...sexual discrimination...

Yuta Okawa Once, I heard that you were very conservative about sexual problems.

King [*Coughs. Drinks water.*] We know about [*coughs*] Sodom and Gomorrah in the Old Testament [*coughs*].

それに加えて別種の差別があります。「性差別」と言うべきもので、略してLGBTと呼ばれる、レズビアン、ゲイ、バイセクシュアル（両性愛者）、トランスジェンダー（性同一性障害など、心と体の性が一致しない人）のことです。

キング牧師　それは、また別の難しい問題ですね。

市川　また別の複雑な差別問題です。こうした、人種差別や性差別などの差別に関して、どうお考えでしょうか。将来に向けて、何らかの解決策がありますでしょうか。

キング牧師　うーん。私の仕事は「人種差別」のほうだったので、うーん……「性差別」ですか。

大川裕太　性的な問題に関しては、あなたは非常に保守的だったと聞いたことがあります。

キング牧師　（咳こむ。水を飲む）旧約聖書の「ソドムとゴモラ」なら（咳）知ってますけどね。ああいった滅亡し

I imagine that kind of ruined city. If men and women abandon their dignity, they cannot be saved by God. I guess so.

So, the sexual problem might be the problem of an affluent society. An affluent society has enough money, enough time and too many chances, so people want to do something different to make some other human history on their own.

So, I cannot follow that kind of lesbian, gay, bisexual and transgender. Uh-huh. Hmm…the word coming from the bottom of my heart is, "No." So, is it good? Do they have a future? Do they live in the future society? Is it freedom? Is it liberty? Is it utopia? I don't think so.

Ishikawa In America, the Supreme Court declared that marriage is a fundamental right for gays and lesbians that cannot be deprived of.

た都市を想像してしまいます。(咳)男女の尊厳が失われたら、神の救いは得られないんじゃないでしょうか。

　まあ、そういう性に関する問題は、「豊かな社会」の問題なのかもしれません。「豊かな社会」はお金と時間が余っていて、いろんなチャンスもあり過ぎるくらいですから、何か違うことがしたくなるんですよ。自分たちで"別の人類史"を作ってみたくなるんでしょう。

　そういうレズビアン、ゲイ、バイセクシュアル、トランスジェンダーまでは、私はついていけません。うーん……心の底から出て来る言葉は「ノー」ですね。いいことなのか。彼らに未来はあるのか。そういう人たちは未来社会にも生きているのか。それが自由なのか。ユートピアなのか。そうは思えませんね。

石川　アメリカの最高裁判所は、「結婚は、ゲイやレズビアンから剝奪されるべからざる基本的人権である」という判決を下しましたが。

King They are bad. Judges are bad. Bad judgment.

Yuta Okawa The main supporters of the Democratic Party, including Barack Obama, tend to support such sexual minorities.

King Oh…Christian people must obey God's rule. God forbids that kind of, how do I say, not-so-beautiful way of life. So, I hate that kind of society. Do you mean marriage between man and man, woman and woman? Oh, no. No.

Yuta Okawa If this is rude I apologize to you, but actually, one historical researcher said you also had a male friend who you loved…

King Oh, of course, I love everyone.

キング牧師 それは、ひどい。ひどい裁判官で、ひどい判決です。

大川裕太 民主党の中心的支持層やバラク・オバマは、そうした性的少数者を支持する傾向にあります。

キング牧師 おお……キリスト教徒は神の掟に従わねばなりません。神は、そういった何と言うか、うーん、あまり美しくない生き方は禁じておられますので。そんな社会は嫌ですね。男同士、女同士で結婚ですか。いや、ノー、ノーです。

大川裕太 失礼であればお詫びいたしますが、実は、ある歴史研究家が、あなたにも愛した男性の友人がいたのではないかと述べています。

キング牧師 ああ、それはそうですよ。誰であっても愛してますから。

Yuta Okawa And he and you were very intimate... even in the night, one historical researcher said.

King [*Laughs.*] You studied a lot.

Yuta Okawa Sorry, I'm so sorry.

King Studying too much! Too much! He was a close friend and not boyfriend, husband or wife.

Yuta Okawa OK. I'm so sorry.

Solve gun control issue by learning from Japan

Ishikawa Can I ask a different question?

King You like men also?

大川裕太　彼とあなたは、夜にも、非常に親密に……。そう言っている歴史研究家がいますが。

キング牧師　（笑）よく勉強してますね。

大川裕太　申し訳ございません。

キング牧師　しすぎです！　勉強しすぎ！　親しい友人ですよ。彼氏とか夫とか妻とかじゃないので。

大川裕太　分かりました。大変申し訳ありませんでした。

銃社会の問題は日本に学んで解決を

石川　別の質問をしてもよろしいでしょうか。

キング牧師　あなたも男性が好きなわけですか。

Ishikawa No, no, no [*laughs*]. I would like to ask about the issue of gun control.

King Gun control?

Ishikawa Yes. Ordinary citizens are gunned down by crazy men and President Obama…

King I was killed by gun.

Ishikawa I think President Obama wants to tighten the gun control and conduct background checks for…

King It's bad, it's against the amendments of the U.S. Constitution. American people can protect themselves by guns, so it's against the constitution. It's a difficult question. It's from the American Frontier, so I cannot definitely say, but gun control is a good thing.

But we must learn from the Japanese. Japanese people are very wise and are living very peacefully

石川　いえいえ、違います（笑）。銃規制問題について伺いたいと思います。

キング牧師　銃規制ね。

石川　はい。一般市民が、狂気じみた男に銃で撃たれ、オバマ大統領は……。

キング牧師　私も銃で殺されましたからね。

石川　オバマ大統領は、銃規制を強化し、身元確認を行いたいと考えていると思います……。

キング牧師　それは、まずいですね。合衆国憲法修正条項に反しています。米国民は銃で自らを護ることができるので、それは憲法違反ですよ。難しい問題ですね。アメリカの開拓時代から来ていることなので、はっきりしたことは言えませんが、銃規制そのものはいいことです。
　ただ、日本人に学ばないといけません。日本人は大変賢明で、お互い平和に生きていますので、日本から学ぶべき

with each other, so it's time to learn from Japan. Japan is a teacher of the world. You can teach us how to live peacefully. Obama is looking at Japan, to the East or the West? I don't know, but he is looking at Japan. Japan is a peaceful society, so it's one ideal society. I support that thinking.

6 Terrorism and the U.S. Presidential Election

Yuta Okawa I would like to ask you about the relationship between racial discrimination and terrorism. Recently, not only in the United States but also in Europe, terrorism is a hot issue.

King I know, I know.

Yuta Okawa I think your hope was the reconciliation among many races. But actually, in reality, segregation is now advancing and sometimes such racial segregation

ときが来ています。日本は「世界の先生役」ですから、平和に生きる方法を教えてください。オバマは日本を見ています。東を見ています、西かな？　分かりませんが、日本を見ています。日本は平和な社会であり、一つの理想的な社会です。そういう考え方を支持したいですね。

6　テロと米大統領選について

大川裕太　人種差別とテロの関係について、お伺いしたいと思います。最近、アメリカだけでなくヨーロッパでも、テロリズムが大きな問題になっています。

キング牧師　そうですね、知っています。

大川裕太　あなたは、人種間の和解を願われていたと思いますが、現実には隔離(かくり)が進んでいます。そうした人種差別が「憎しみ」を加速させる場合もあり、最終的に、テロと

accelerates hatred and finally, results in terrorism. So, how can we overcome this situation or extreme hatred?

A bridge is needed between the religious philosophies of America and the Middle East

King I cannot agree with terrorism. It is the separation or the difference between Malcolm X* and I. Mahatma Gandhi in India and I don't like such kind of violence. Violence attracts violence only. I can imagine and guess the jihad of the Islamic people and how they have been attacked by the modern American or European army. It's a very severe and hard attack, I think. So, if it's a new Crusade, they must fight against that kind of force.

But today, the difference between Islamic countries and America or Europe, the EU, is very huge. If they want to continue such kind of killing by using

---

* An African-American civil rights activist (1925-1965). He is known for his radical actions, as opposed to King who advocated nonviolence. Spiritual messages from Malcolm X were recorded two days after King's.

いう結果になっています。こうした状況や行き過ぎた憎しみを乗り越えるには、どうすればいいのでしょうか。

米国と中東の宗教思想には「橋渡し」が必要

キング牧師 テロには賛成できません。そこがマルコムX（注）と私を分ける点であり、違いです。私も、インドのマハトマ・ガンジーも、その種の暴力は好みません。暴力は暴力を招くだけです。イスラム教徒のジハード（聖戦）は想像がつきます。彼らはアメリカやヨーロッパの近代的な軍隊によって攻撃されてきました。非常に厳しく激しい攻撃だったでしょう。ですから、これが"新たな十字軍"であるなら、そういう勢力とは戦わなければなりません。

　ところが今日では、「イスラム諸国」と「アメリカやヨーロッパ、EU」の間には、ものすごい差があります。子供とか母親とか、普通の人を使って相手を殺し続けようとす

（注）アメリカの黒人公民権運動活動家（1925〜65）。非暴力を掲げたキングとは対照的に、過激な活動で知られる。本霊言の二日後、マルコムXの霊言が収録された。

children, mothers or common people like that, it's bad from the viewpoint of God. And if they make horror or terrible scenes in Europe or the United States, it may invite another massive attack like the Gulf War or the Iraq War.

So, I want to say and I want to advocate that American president should make a declaration, "Stop terrorism and we will not attack you by modern technology or modern scientific army." It's not fair. America has a lot of latest weapons. They cannot fight against America or the EU. Using humans as a weapon is not so good. They should stop and hold conversations between them.

Maybe people in the Middle East area have a lot of pride in their history and culture, so they degrade American people as a younger country with only 200 or 300 years of history. They have thousands of years of history and they have worshiped God. They think that American people don't have any God. "American people only have Avengers and X-MEN. American

るなら、それは、神の視点からは「悪」です。ヨーロッパやアメリカで身の毛もよだつ悲惨な光景を繰り広げるのであれば、湾岸戦争やイラク戦争のような、新たな大規模攻撃を招くことになるかもしれません。

ですから、私はこう申し上げたい、主張したい。アメリカ大統領は、「テロをやめよ。そうすれば、われわれも近代技術や現代科学を擁する軍隊による攻撃は加えない」と宣言すべきです。不公平ですよ。アメリカには最新兵器が豊富にありますので、アメリカやEUと戦うのは無理です。"人間兵器"は、よくありません。それはやめて、対話をすべきです。

中東の人々は、自分たちの歴史や文化に自信満々なので、アメリカ人を、ほんの二、三百年の歴史しかない若い国だと思って、低く見てるんじゃないでしょうかね。彼らには数千年の歴史があり、神を崇拝してきました。彼らは、「アメリカ国民には神がいない」と思っているのです。「アベンジャーズやX‐MENしかいない。アメリカ人には神がいない。イラクやイラン、サウジアラビア、エジプトなど

people have no God. But for example, Iraqi people, Iranian people, Saudi or Egyptian people have God, Allah. We have a God to worship, but America only has heroes." So, they think American people don't know the difference between God and heroes. Hero is the starting point of one of gods, but they think, "America has a shallow history, so with the short history they don't have a proper God. America has no God," so they look down upon America. This is the problem.

America looks down upon such kind of African continent and the western Asian countries, thinking that their God is Mammon*, I mean the Satan-like God. Old god who controls and uses people as he likes, I mean like robots or animals.

Only God has sovereignty. Do you understand the word, *sovereignty*? It's a country's governing power. In the western countries, the power of the nations

---

* In the New Testament, mammon means "wealth." It is used to mean, "god of money."

の人々には神すなわちアッラーがいて崇拝しているが、アメリカにはヒーローしかいない」と。「アメリカ人は神とヒーローの違いが分からない」と思っているわけです。ヒーロー（英雄）は"神々の始まり"なのですが、「アメリカは歴史が浅いから、ちゃんとした神はいない。アメリカには神がいない」と思ってアメリカを見下しているのです。ここが問題です。

アメリカのほうは、アフリカ大陸や西アジアの国々に対して、「彼らの神はマモン（注）である」、要するにサタンのような神であるとして見下しています。人間を支配して、ロボットや動物みたいに自分の好きにする、古い神です。

「神にしか主権はない」というわけです。「主権」という言葉はお分かりですか。国を治める権力のことです。西洋諸国では、国家の権力は国民一人ひとりに由来します。そ

（注）新約聖書において「富」を意味する言葉。金銭の神の意味で用いられる。

comes from every citizen. This is the sovereign power of the democratic countries. But some of the Asian and African people just rely on one God, for example Allah. Allah is the only one, the almighty one. And people are like ants. They are equal, but they are ants. It's not the democratic style of thinking.

This is the American view of the people of West Asia, that they are ruled by Mammon, I mean the god of money in the ancient age. In the true meaning, it's an evil spirit or a demon. They are worshiping a demon. This is, in reality, the American standard. But you, Japanese new religion, are building a new bridge between two sides, Allah and Jesus Christ. So, it is a very important job. Please lead them in a good direction.

"America First" vs. "Lady First"

Ishikawa The presidential election will be held in November, so I would like to ask one more question. Donald Trump's policy is, "America First."

れが民主主義国の主権ですけれども、アジアやアフリカの人々の一部は、唯一の神、例えばアッラーに頼るだけなんです。アッラーが「一なる者」であり全能であって、人間は蟻に過ぎません。平等ではあるけれども蟻なんです。これは民主主義的な考え方ではありません。

アメリカは西アジアの人々をそんなふうに見ているわけです。古代の金銭の神であるマモンに支配されていると。実際は悪霊あるいは悪魔なんですがね。彼らは悪魔崇拝をしているというのがアメリカ標準の見方なんですが、日本の新しい宗教であるあなた方は、アッラーとイエス・キリスト、両者の間に"新たな橋"を架けようとしていますので、非常に重要な仕事です。ぜひ、彼らをいい方向へ導いていってください。

「アメリカ・ファースト」vs.「レディー・ファースト」

石川　１１月に大統領選がありますので、もう一つお伺いしたいのですが、ドナルド・トランプの政策は「アメリカ第一」です。これは神のご意志にかなっているでしょうか。

Is this in accordance with God's will? A little too straightforward?

King I'm not a politician and I'm not a journalist, and their policies may change in the near future. I cannot say exactly the difference between Donald Trump and Hillary Clinton. Hillary Clinton's age will be the "Age of Women." Maybe around 40 percent of executives in American companies or administrators in the government will be women. This will be the age of Hillary Clinton. It is one part of equality.

But Donald Trump will change the American bureaucrats. In the English meaning, *bureaucrat* means, as you know, incapability. People who are incapable are bureaucrats. American bureaucrats use a lot of money in a different way, so he will change this point. He is a businessman, so he can change the budget system, tax system and the law system. If he succeeds, people will be grateful for his deed.

And Hillary Clinton wants to break through the

少しストレート過ぎる質問かもしれませんが。

キング牧師 私は政治家でもジャーナリストでもありませんし、彼らの政策も近い将来、変わるかもしれませんので、ドナルド・トランプとヒラリー・クリントンの違いに関して正確なことは言えませんが、ヒラリー・クリントンの時代は「女性の時代」になるでしょう。企業や政府の管理職の４０％程度は女性になるというのがヒラリー・クリントンの時代でしょう。これは平等の一側面です。

　しかしドナルド・トランプは、アメリカの官僚（bureaucrat）を変えるでしょう。英語では、bureaucratとは「無能」という意味ですので。無能な人々、それが官僚です。アメリカの官僚は違った方面に莫大な金を使っていますから、彼はこの点を変えるでしょうね。彼はビジネスマンですから、予算制度や税制や法制度を変えていけます。これに成功すれば、感謝されるでしょう。

　ヒラリー・クリントンは"ガラスの天井"、すなわち女

glass ceiling, meaning the discrimination against women. It's one historical challenge. But as you know, a weaker America cannot save the world. If the world, I mean the 200 countries want America to be great and save the world, this can be the point. However, at this time, Mr. Donald Trump thinks America first, so it is isolationism. And Hillary is lady first. So, "America First" or "Lady First" [*audience laughs*], these two choices. It's very difficult. I want to choose a third candidate [*laughs*].

Yuta Okawa From your viewpoint, is President Barack Obama a good person? Does he reflect God's will? Is he a good person for the United States?

King He has a religious personality, I think. He's a good man. But is he a capable person or not? I don't know exactly because the super power of America is declining. So, is it good for the world or not? I cannot say exactly.

性に対する差別を破りたがっています。これは一つの歴史的挑戦ですが、ご存じの通り、アメリカが弱くなれば世界を救えなくなります。世界の２００カ国が、偉大なアメリカに世界を救ってほしいなら、ここがポイントになってきます。ドナルド・トランプ氏は現時点で「アメリカ第一」を考えていますので、これは孤立主義です。ヒラリーのほうはレディー・ファーストですから、「アメリカ・ファースト」か「レディー・ファースト」か（会場笑）、この二択です。実に難しい。第三の候補者を選びたくなりますよ（笑）。

大川裕太　あなたからご覧になって、バラク・オバマ大統領は善人ですか。神の意志を反映しているのでしょうか。アメリカにとって好ましい人物でしょうか。

キング牧師　宗教的な人格の方だと思います。善人ではありますが、有能かどうかは、よく分かりません。アメリカの強大な力が衰えてきていますので。世界にとっていいことかどうか、明確には言えません。

7 The Secret of Dr. King's Soul

Ichikawa I'm sorry to ask you about a spiritual secret…

King Secret?

Ichikawa Yes, a spiritual secret, as you are now a spiritual being.

King Spiritual secret!?

Past life is a person in the Old Testament

Ichikawa Your preachings were so powerful and your vibration was so inspiring. Do you have any strong spiritual connection with any high spirits in Heaven or are you a part of a spiritual being in Heaven? Do you understand my question?

7　キング牧師の魂の秘密

市川　恐れ入りますが、霊的秘密についてお伺いしたいと思います。

キング牧師　秘密？

市川　はい、霊的秘密です。現在は霊存在でいらっしゃいますので。

キング牧師　霊的秘密とは⁉

過去世は旧約聖書中の人物

市川　あなたの説教はたいへん力強く、人を鼓舞(こぶ)する強いバイブレーションがありました。ですので、どなたか天上界の高級霊と、何らかの霊的な深い縁がおありなのでしょうか。あるいは、天上界の霊存在の一部でいらっしゃるのでしょうか。質問の意味は、ご理解いただけますか。

King Yeah, I understand.

Ichikawa To be very straightforward, your vibration is quite like Jesus Christ. Do you have any strong relationship with Jesus Christ?

King I am one of the prophets. Yeah. One of the prophets. Maybe you know or you don't know, I'm not sure. Do you know Malachi? Prophet Malachi*?

Ichikawa So, your past life was Malachi?

King Yeah. Malachi.

Yuta Okawa Your past incarnation was Malachi?

* A prophet of the Northern Kingdom of Israel. He is the author of the *Book of Malachi* in the Old Testament. [Picture from the 14th century, Italy.]

7　キング牧師の魂の秘密

キング牧師　ええ、分かりますよ。

市川　率直(そっちょく)に申し上げると、あなたの波動はイエス・キリストによく似ています。イエス・キリストと深い縁がおありなのでしょうか。

キング牧師　私は預言者(よげんしゃ)の一人なんです。ええ。預言者の一人です。ご存じかどうか分かりませんが、マラキという人はご存じですか。預言者マラキ（注）です。

市川　では、過去世はマラキでいらっしゃるのですか。

キング牧師　ええ、マラキです。

大川裕太　過去には、マラキとしてお生まれになったわけですか。

（注）旧約聖書「マラキ書」で知られる、北イスラエル王国の預言者（写真は１４世紀イタリアの絵画）。

King Yeah.

Yuta Okawa Prophet Malachi. Do you have any other historical names in your spirit?

King Recently? Hmm…recently. Recently, recently… Maybe I can't say exactly, but I'm friends with Mr. President Lincoln or Shotoku Taishi of Japan. And other people…

Yuta Okawa Solon* in Ancient Greece?

King Solon…I'm poor, so… maybe not.

Yuta Okawa Lincoln's incarnation.

---

* An ancient Greek statesman and lawmaker. He is one of the seven sages of Greece. Solon is believed to have laid the foundations of Athenian democracy. Refer to Chapter 2 of *The Golden Laws* [New York: IRH Press, 2015] in regards to his later incarnations.

7　キング牧師の魂の秘密

キング牧師　はい。

大川裕太　預言者マラキですね。他に魂の中で、歴史にお名前が遺(のこ)っている方はいますか。

キング牧師　最近ですか。うーん……最近。最近、最近……。たぶん、はっきりとは分かりませんが、リンカン大統領か日本の聖徳太子の友人かもしれません。そのほかでは……。

大川裕太　古代ギリシャのソロン（注）ですか。

キング牧師　ソロン……。私は貧しいので、たぶん違うでしょう。

大川裕太　リンカンの生まれ変わりの。

（注）紀元前7〜6世紀の古代ギリシャの政治家・立法者で、ギリシャ七賢人の一人。アテネの民主主義の基礎を築いたとされる。彼の転生に関しては『黄金の法』（大川隆法著、幸福の科学出版刊）第2章参照。

King Lincoln? Oh, yeah. That's good.

Yuta Okawa Lincoln's past incarnation was Solon in Greece.

King Oh, maybe a no-name person who was killed on the cross. Maybe a no-name saint.

Ishikawa You were persecuted by Emperor Nero or…

King Ah, a lot of Christian people were killed, so maybe one of them.

Yuta Okawa I guess you were also born as an African person…

King Ah, maybe.

Yuta Okawa Do you have any other incarnation in Africa or ancient Egypt? If all your reincarnations were

キング牧師　リンカン？　おお、それは素晴らしい。

大川裕太　リンカンの過去世はギリシャのソロンでした。

キング牧師　ああ、十字架にかかって殺された無名の人かもしれませんね。無名の聖人かもしれません。

石川　ネロ帝に迫害された人であるとか……。

キング牧師　ああ、キリスト教徒で殺された人は多かったので、そのうちの一人かもしれません。

大川裕太　アフリカ人としても、お生まれになったのではありませんか。

キング牧師　ああ、かもしれません。

大川裕太　アフリカや古代エジプトなどに転生されたことはございますか。あなたの転生が白人ばかりだと、黒人の

white people, black people would be disappointed in some cases.

King Human race has a long, long history. In Africa, there are a lot of countries, a lot of religions and a lot of religious leaders in history. Almost all of them are forgotten in the wave of history, and I have many experiences too, of course. But every time, I was a religious leader and every time, or sometimes, I was killed.

"I invited my death"

Ishikawa I have one more question. In your last speech, you said, "I've seen the Promised Land. I may not get there with you*." So, on the night before your assassination, did you foresee your destiny?

---

* King delivered an address, "I've Been to the Mountaintop," on April 3, 1968, in Memphis, Tennessee. Near the end of the address, he said, "Like anybody, I would like to live a long life. Longevity has its place. But I'm not concerned about that now." "I've seen the Promised Land. I may not get there with you." These lines are well known, as many people think that he foresaw his assassination on the following day, April 4.

方が、がっかりする場合もあるかもしれませんので。

キング牧師 人類には長い長い歴史があるんです。アフリカには多くの国があり、歴史上、多くの宗教があり、大勢の宗教家がいました。そのほとんどは歴史の波間に忘れ去られていますが、当然私にも、数多くの経験があるんです。ただ、私はいつの時代も宗教家でしたし、いつの時代も、いえ、ある時代には、殺されてきました。

「私の死は自ら招いたもの」

石川 もう一つ質問があります。あなたは最後となった演説の中で、「私は約束の地を見た。あなたがたと共に辿り着くことはできないかもしれない」と言われました（注）。つまり、暗殺される前の晩に、ご自分の運命を予見されていたのでしょうか。

（注）1968年4月3日、テネシー州メンフィスで行われた演説「I've Been to the Mountaintop（私は山頂に達した）」のこと。演説の最後には「長生きをするのも悪くないが、今の私にはどうでもいい。（中略）私は約束の地を見た。あなたがたと共に辿り着くことはできないかもしれない。」とあり、翌4月4日の自身の暗殺を予見したかのような内容で有名。

King My destiny?

Ishikawa Next day, I think you were assassinated.

King What do you mean? Just that day?

Yuta Okawa Just the day before your death, you gave a speech.

Ishikawa And in that speech you said, "I may not get there with you," so some people guess you foresaw your destiny before your assassination.

King Yeah. Hmm…It…It came true. I invited my death. I wanted to stand by Jesus Christ. Jesus Christ was crucified, killed by the people who were loved by Jesus and who persecuted Jesus. So, I welcomed to be killed. I wanted to sit near Jesus Christ, so I welcomed my death.

キング牧師　運命をですか。

石川　翌日、暗殺されたかと思いますので。

キング牧師　どういう意味ですか。その日ですか。

大川裕太　死の前日に、演説をされました。

石川　その演説で、「あなたがたと共に辿り着くことはできないかもしれない」とおっしゃったので、暗殺の前に運命を予見していたのではないかと推測している人もいます。

キング牧師　はい。うーん……それは……実現してしまいましたね。私の死は自ら招いたものなのです。イエス・キリストのお側に立ちたかったのです。イエス・キリストは十字架に架けられ、イエスに愛された人々や、イエスを迫害した人々によって殺されました。ですから私も、殺されることを歓迎していました。イエス・キリストの傍近くに座りたかったので、自らの死を歓迎していたんですよ。

Friends in Heaven

Yuta Okawa May I ask one more question? Is Mahatma Gandhi or Nelson Mandela your friend in Heaven?

King Yeah, my friends. My friends.

Yuta Okawa OK. OK, thank you very much.

King [*To Yuta Okawa.*] And you are my friend.

Yuta Okawa Thank you very much. Do you have any other friends in Heaven?

King You are my Japanese friend.

Yuta Okawa Thank you very much.

King My Japanese friend, yeah. You and Shotoku Taishi

天上界での友人たち

大川裕太　もう一つ質問してもよろしいでしょうか。マハトマ・ガンジーやネルソン・マンデラは、天上界で、あなたのご友人ですか。

キング牧師　はい、友人です。友人です。

大川裕太　分かりました。ありがとうございます。

キング牧師　（大川裕太に）あなたとも友人ですよ。

大川裕太　ありがとうございます。他にも、天上界で友人がいらっしゃるでしょうか。

キング牧師　あなたが日本の友人です。

大川裕太　どうもありがとうございます。

キング牧師　日本の友人です。そう。あなたと聖徳太子が

are my friends. And Amaterasu-O-Mikami is also my friend. They are truly my friends.

And Jesus Christ is a very close friend of Ryuho Okawa. Jesus Christ comes to this house or chapel, I don't know. He should go to church, but he usually doesn't go to church. He comes to Happy Science church or Happy Science Master's house and sometimes gives advice to Master Okawa. He's a close friend of Master Okawa.

Maybe, I just guess, but maybe he is one part of Master Okawa. He is the right foot or the right hand of Master Okawa, I think. Almost 30 percent of the doctrines of Happy Science come from Jesus Christ, I've heard. So, he is a part of the power of Master Ryuho Okawa. I think so.

Yuta Okawa Thank you very much.

友人です。天照大神(あまてらすおおみかみ)もそうです。本当ですよ。

　イエス・キリストは、大川隆法の大変親しい友人です。イエス・キリストは、この"家"というのか"教会"なのか、分かりませんが、ここに来られます。イエス・キリストはキリスト教会に行かないといけないのですが、普通は行ってません。イエス・キリストは幸福の科学の教会や、幸福の科学の教祖殿に来て、大川総裁にアドバイスしていることもあります。イエスは大川総裁とは親しい友人です。

　たぶん、推測に過ぎませんが、イエスは大川総裁の一部、「右足」か「右手」ではないかと思います。幸福の科学の教義の三割くらいはイエス・キリストから来ていると聞いていますので、彼は"大川隆法総裁の力の一部"なのだと思いますね。

大川裕太　ありがとうございます。

8 A New Dream for America and the World

Ichikawa Thank you very much. So, as a conclusion, if you were in the United States of America now, what kind of dream would you realize? This is our last request. What kind of dream do you want to realize?

King Oh…

> People are equally treated
> In spite of their colors or their original countries.
> And people are very merciful and
> Loving other people without violence.
> And truly, truly believing in God.
>
> I now realize that one part of Master Ryuho Okawa
> Is God Thoth*, who has sovereignty

---

* A great spiritual leader who built the golden age of the Atlantis civilization around 12,000 years ago. He was known as the god of wisdom in ancient Egypt, and is also the branch spirit of the God of the Earth, El Cantare.

8　アメリカと世界の新たな夢

市川　ありがとうございます。それでは最後に、もし、あなたが今アメリカにいらっしゃるとしたら、どんな夢を実現されるでしょうか。これが最後の質問です。どんな夢を実現したいと思われますか。

キング牧師　ああ……。
　人々が、肌の色や生まれた国にかかわらず
　平等な扱いを受けること。
　慈悲深く、暴力を振るうことなく、
　人を愛すること。
　そして、心から、心から、神を信じていること。

　大川隆法総裁の一部が
　北米大陸を統(す)べておられるトス神(しん)（注）であると、

(注) 約1万2千年前にアトランティス文明の最盛期を築いた大導師。古代エジプトでは知恵の神として知られていた。地球神エル・カンターレの分身である。

Over the North American continent.
So, this teaching of Happy Science
Will save all the world.
It's not a Japanese religion.
It's a world religion.

May people be peaceful.
May people love each other.
May people be wealthy and healthy,
And without violence,
Build a new Utopia in the near future.
I hope so.

Yuta Okawa Thank you very much.

Ichikawa So, this concludes the spiritual message from Dr. Martin Luther King, Jr. Thank you very much.

今、分かりました。
ですから、この幸福の科学の教えが
全世界を救うでしょう。
これは日本の宗教ではありません。
世界宗教なのです。

人々の間に平和がありますように。
人々が互いに愛し合いますように。
人々が豊かで健(すこ)やかでありますように。
暴力に訴えることなく、遠くない未来において
新たなユートピアを築くことができますように。
それを願っています。

大川裕太　ありがとうございます。

市川　それでは以上で、マーティン・ルーサー・キング・ジュニア牧師の霊言を終了いたします。ありがとうございました。

After receiving the spiritual messages

Ryuho Okawa Thank you very much. [*Claps three times.*] Hmm… well spoken. He said a lot. Is it enough?

Yuta Okawa Yes. Thank you very much.

Ichikawa Thank you very much.

Yuta Okawa And his last message was very strong for American people. Actually, Happy Science is sometimes considered as a Japanese religion. It's not. It's a very sensitive problem for white American people to believe in a Japanese god. But his message was very strong. And for American people, Happy Science will be considered as a great religion.

Ryuho Okawa Thank you, Dr. Martin Luther King, Jr. [*Claps once.*] Thank you, thank you very much.

8　アメリカと世界の新たな夢

霊言を終えて

大川隆法　ありがとうございました。(手を三回叩く。)はい。立派な言葉でした。いろいろ話してくれましたね。十分でしたか。

大川裕太　はい。ありがとうございました。

市川　ありがとうございました。

大川裕太　彼の最後のメッセージは、アメリカ人に対して非常に力があります。実際、幸福の科学は日本の宗教として捉えられてしまうことがあります。そうではないのです。白人のアメリカ人にとって、日本の神を信じるのは、けっこう微妙(びみょう)な問題なのですが、彼のメッセージは非常に力強かったので、アメリカ人にも、幸福の科学は偉大な宗教として見られることになると思います。

大川隆法　ありがとう、マーティン・ルーサー・キング・ジュニア牧師。(手を一回叩く)ありがとうございました。

『キング牧師　天国からのメッセージ』
大川隆法著作関連書籍

『正義の法』　　　　　　　　　　（幸福の科学出版刊）
『黄金の法』　　　　　　　　　　　　　　　　（同）

『キング牧師 天国からのメッセージ』
―アメリカの課題と夢―

2016年9月29日　初版第1刷

著　者　　大川隆法

発行所　　幸福の科学出版株式会社

〒107-0052　東京都港区赤坂2丁目10番14号
TEL(03) 5573-7700
http://www.irhpress.co.jp/

印刷・製本　　株式会社 堀内印刷所

落丁・乱丁本はおとりかえいたします
©Ryuho Okawa 2016. Printed in Japan. 検印省略
ISBN 978-4-86395-839-5 C0014
Photo：AP/アフロ／時事／CNP／時事通信フォト

大川隆法ベストセラーズ・英語説法&世界の指導者の本心

Power to the Future
未来に力を

英語説法集 日本語訳付き

予断を許さない日本の国防危機。混迷を極める世界情勢の行方――。ワールド・ティーチャーが英語で語った、この国と世界の進むべき道とは。

1,400円

守護霊インタビュー ドナルド・トランプ アメリカ復活への戦略

英語霊言 日本語訳付き

次期アメリカ大統領を狙う不動産王の知られざる素顔とは? 過激な発言を繰り返しても支持率トップを走る「ドナルド旋風」の秘密に迫る!

1,400円

オバマ大統領の 新・守護霊メッセージ

日中韓問題、TPP交渉、ウクライナ問題、安倍首相への要望……。来日直前のオバマ大統領の本音に迫った、緊急守護霊インタビュー!

英語霊言 日本語訳付き

1,400円

幸福の科学出版

大川隆法ベストセラーズ・世界の指導者の本心

ヒラリー・クリントンの政治外交リーディング
同盟国から見た日本外交の問題点

竹島、尖閣と続発する日本の領土問題……。国防意識なき同盟国をアメリカはどう見ているのか? クリントン国務長官の本心に迫る!
【幸福実現党刊】

1,400円

ネルソン・マンデラ ラスト・メッセージ

英語霊言 日本語訳付き

人種差別と戦い、27年もの投獄に耐え、民族融和の理想を貫いた偉大なる指導者ネルソン・マンデラ。その「復活」のメッセージを全世界の人びとに!

1,400円

イラク戦争は正しかったか
サダム・フセインの死後を霊査する

全世界衝撃の公開霊言。「大量破壊兵器は存在した!」「9.11はフセインが計画し、ビン・ラディンが実行した!」——。驚愕の事実が明らかに。

1,400円

※表示価格は本体価格(税別)です。

大川隆法 ベストセラーズ・世界の指導者の本心

プーチン 日本の政治を叱る

緊急守護霊メッセージ

日本はロシアとの友好を失ってよいのか? 日露首脳会談の翌日、優柔不断な日本の政治を一刀両断する、プーチン大統領守護霊の「本音トーク」。

1,400円

守護霊インタビュー
駐日アメリカ大使
キャロライン・ケネディ
日米の新たな架け橋

先の大戦、歴史問題、JFK暗殺の真相……。親日派とされるケネディ駐日米国大使の守護霊が語る、日本への思いと日米の未来。

1,400円

サッチャーの
スピリチュアル・メッセージ
死後19時間での奇跡のインタビュー

フォークランド紛争、英国病、景気回復……。勇気を持って数々の難問を解決し、イギリスを繁栄に導いたサッチャー元首相が、日本にアドバイス!

1,300円

幸福の科学出版

大川隆法ベストセラーズ・世界の指導者の本心

「忍耐の時代」の外交戦略
チャーチルの霊言

もしチャーチルなら、どんな外交戦略を立てるのか？"ヒットラーを倒した男"が語る、ウクライナ問題のゆくえと日米・日ロ外交の未来図とは。

1,400円

イラン大統領
vs.イスラエル首相
中東の核戦争は回避できるのか

英語霊言 日本語訳付き

世界が注視するイランとイスラエルの対立。それぞれのトップの守護霊が、緊迫する中東問題の核心を赤裸々に語る。【幸福実現党刊】

1,400円

アサド大統領の
スピリチュアル・メッセージ

混迷するシリア問題の真相を探るため、アサド大統領の守護霊言に挑む──。恐るべき独裁者の実像が明らかに！

英語霊言 日本語訳付き

1,400円

※表示価格は本体価格(税別)です。

大川隆法「法シリーズ」・最新刊

正義の法
憎しみを超えて、愛を取れ

法シリーズ第22作

テロ事件、中東紛争、中国の軍拡――。
どうすれば世界から争いがなくなるのか。
あらゆる価値観の対立を超える
「正義」とは何か。
著者二千冊目となる「法シリーズ」最新刊！

2,000円

第1章　神は沈黙していない──「学問的正義」を超える「真理」とは何か
第2章　宗教と唯物論の相克──人間の魂を設計したのは誰なのか
第3章　正しさからの発展──「正義」の観点から見た「政治と経済」
第4章　正義の原理
　　　　　　──「個人における正義」と「国家間における正義」の考え方
第5章　人類史の大転換──日本が世界のリーダーとなるために必要なこと
第6章　神の正義の樹立──今、世界に必要とされる「至高神」の教え

幸福の科学出版

大川隆法シリーズ・最新刊

凡事徹底と静寂の時間
現代における"禅的生活"のすすめ

目まぐるしい現代社会のなかで、私たちが失ってはいけない大切なことや、智慧を磨き、人格を向上させる"知的エッセンス"が、この一冊に。

1,500円

蓮舫の守護霊霊言
"民進党イメージ・キャラクター"の正体

蓮舫氏は果たして総理の器なのか? 国防や外交、天皇制、経済政策についてどう考えるのか? 民進党の人気政治家の驚くべき本音が明らかに。【幸福実現党刊】

1,400円

自称"元首"の本心に迫る
安倍首相の守護霊霊言

幸福実現党潰しは、アベノミクスの失速隠しと、先の参院選や都知事選への恨みか? 国民が知らない安倍首相の本音を守護霊が包み隠さず語った。

1,400円

※表示価格は本体価格(税別)です。

幸福の科学グループのご案内

宗教、教育、政治、出版などの活動を通じて、地球的ユートピアの実現を目指しています。

幸福の科学

1986年に立宗。信仰の対象は、地球系霊団の最高大霊、主エル・カンターレ。世界100カ国以上の国々に信者を持ち、全人類救済という尊い使命のもと、信者は、「愛」と「悟り」と「ユートピア建設」の教えの実践、伝道に励んでいます。

（2016年9月現在）

愛

幸福の科学の「愛」とは、与える愛です。これは、仏教の慈悲や布施の精神と同じことです。信者は、仏法真理をお伝えすることを通して、多くの方に幸福な人生を送っていただくための活動に励んでいます。

悟り

「悟り」とは、自らが仏の子であることを知るということです。教学や精神統一によって心を磨き、智慧を得て悩みを解決すると共に、天使・菩薩の境地を目指し、より多くの人を救える力を身につけていきます。

ユートピア建設

私たち人間は、地上に理想世界を建設するという尊い使命を持って生まれてきています。社会の悪を押しとどめ、善を推し進めるために、信者はさまざまな活動に積極的に参加しています。

海外支援・災害支援

国内外の世界で貧困や災害、心の病で苦しんでいる人々に対しては、現地メンバーや支援団体と連携して、物心両面にわたり、あらゆる手段で手を差し伸べています。

自殺を減らそうキャンペーン

年間約3万人の自殺者を減らすため、全国各地で街頭キャンペーンを展開しています。

公式サイト **www.withyou-hs.net**

ヘレンの会

ヘレン・ケラーを理想として活動する、ハンディキャップを持つ方とボランティアの会です。視聴覚障害者、肢体不自由な方々に仏法真理を学んでいただくための、さまざまなサポートをしています。

公式サイト **www.helen-hs.net**

INFORMATION

お近くの精舎・支部・拠点など、お問い合わせは、こちらまで！
幸福の科学サービスセンター
TEL. **03-5793-1727** （受付時間 火〜金：10〜20時／土・日：10〜18時）
幸福の科学公式サイト **happy-science.jp**

幸福の科学グループの教育・人材養成事業

 ハッピー・サイエンス・
ユニバーシティ
Happy Science University

ハッピー・サイエンス・ユニバーシティとは

ハッピー・サイエンス・ユニバーシティ(HSU)は、大川隆法総裁が設立された
「現代の松下村塾」であり、「日本発の本格私学」です。
建学の精神として「幸福の探究と新文明の創造」を掲げ、
チャレンジ精神にあふれ、新時代を切り拓く人材の輩出を目指します。

学部のご案内

人間幸福学部

人間学を学び、新時代を
切り拓くリーダーとなる

経営成功学部

企業や国家の繁栄を実現する、起業家精神あふれる人材となる

未来産業学部

新文明の源流を創造する
チャレンジャーとなる

未来創造学部　2016年4月開設

**時代を変え、
未来を創る主役となる**

政治家やジャーナリスト、ライター、俳優・タレントなどのスター、映画監督・脚本家などのクリエーター人材を育てます。 ※

※キャンパスは東京がメインとなり、2年制の短期特進課程も新設します（4年制の1年次は千葉です）。2017年3月までは、赤坂「ユートピア活動推進館」、2017年4月より東京都江東区（東西線東陽町駅近く）の新校舎「HSU未来創造・東京キャンパス」がキャンパスとなります。

住所　〒299-4325　千葉県長生郡長生村一松丙 4427-1
　　　TEL.0475-32-7770

幸福の科学グループの教育・人材養成事業

教育

学校法人 幸福の科学学園

学校法人 幸福の科学学園は、幸福の科学の教育理念のもとにつくられた教育機関です。人間にとって最も大切な宗教教育の導入を通じて精神性を高めながら、ユートピア建設に貢献する人材輩出を目指しています。

幸福の科学学園

中学校・高等学校（那須本校）
2010年4月開校・栃木県那須郡（男女共学・全寮制）
TEL 0287-75-7777
公式サイト happy-science.ac.jp

関西中学校・高等学校（関西校）
2013年4月開校・滋賀県大津市（男女共学・寮及び通学）
TEL 077-573-7774
公式サイト kansai.happy-science.ac.jp

仏法真理塾「サクセスNo.1」 TEL 03-5750-0747（東京本校）
小・中・高校生が、信仰教育を基礎にしながら、「勉強も『心の修行』」と考えて学んでいます。

不登校児支援スクール「ネバー・マインド」 TEL 03-5750-1741
心の面からのアプローチを重視して、不登校の子供たちを支援しています。
また、障害児支援の「ユー・アー・エンゼル！」運動も行っています。

エンゼルプランV TEL 03-5750-0757
幼少時からの心の教育を大切にして、信仰をベースにした幼児教育を行っています。

シニア・プラン21 TEL 03-6384-0778
希望に満ちた生涯現役人生のために、年齢を問わず、多くの方が学んでいます。

NPO活動支援

学校からのいじめ追放を目指し、さまざまな社会提言をしています。また、各地でのシンポジウムや学校への啓発ポスター掲示等に取り組む一般財団法人「いじめから子供を守ろうネットワーク」を支援しています。

公式サイト mamoro.org
ブログ blog.mamoro.org
相談窓口 TEL.03-5719-2170

幸福の科学グループ事業

政治

幸福実現党

内憂外患(ないゆうがいかん)の国難に立ち向かうべく、2009年5月に幸福実現党を立党しました。創立者である大川隆法党総裁の精神的指導のもと、宗教だけでは解決できない問題に取り組み、幸福を具体化するための力になっています。

幸福実現党 釈量子サイト
shaku-ryoko.net

釈量子@shakuryoko
で検索

党の機関紙
「幸福実現NEWS」

幸福実現党 党員募集中

あなたも幸福を実現する政治に参画しませんか。

○ 幸福実現党の理念と綱領、政策に賛同する18歳以上の方なら、どなたでも党員になることができます。
○ 党員の期間は、党費（年額 一般党員5,000円、学生党員2,000円）を入金された日から1年間となります。

党員になると

党員限定の機関紙が送付されます（学生党員の方にはメールにてお送りします）。申込書は、下記、幸福実現党公式サイトでダウンロードできます。

住所 〒107-0052
東京都港区赤坂2-10-8 6階
幸福実現党本部

TEL 03-6441-0754
FAX 03-6441-0764
公式サイト **hr-party.jp**
若者向け政治サイト **truthyouth.jp**

幸福の科学グループ事業

アー・ユー・ハッピー？
are-you-happy.com

ザ・リバティ
the-liberty.com

幸福の科学出版

大川隆法総裁の仏法真理の書を中心に、ビジネス、自己啓発、小説など、さまざまなジャンルの書籍・雑誌を出版しています。他にも、映画事業、文学・学術発展のための振興事業、テレビ・ラジオ番組の提供など、幸福の科学文化を広げる事業を行っています。

幸福の科学出版
TEL 03-5573-7700
公式サイト **irhpress.co.jp**

ザ・ファクト
マスコミが報道しない「事実」を世界に伝えるネット・オピニオン番組

Youtubeにて随時好評配信中！

ザ・ファクト 検索

ニュースター・プロダクション

ニュースター・プロダクション（株）は、新時代の"美しさ"を創造する芸能プロダクションです。2016年3月には、ニュースター・プロダクション製作映画「天使に"アイム・ファイン"」を公開しました。

公式サイト
newstar-pro.com

入 会 の ご 案 内

あなたも、幸福の科学に集い、ほんとうの幸福を見つけてみませんか？

幸福の科学では、大川隆法総裁が説く仏法真理をもとに、
「どうすれば幸福になれるのか、また、
他の人を幸福にできるのか」を学び、実践しています。

入会

大川隆法総裁の教えを信じ、学ぼうとする方なら、どなたでも入会できます。入会された方には、『入会版「正心法語」』が授与されます。（入会の奉納は1,000円目安です）

ネットでも入会できます。詳しくは、下記URLへ。
happy-science.jp/joinus

三帰誓願

仏弟子としてさらに信仰を深めたい方は、仏・法・僧の三宝への帰依を誓う「三帰誓願式」を受けることができます。三帰誓願者には、『仏説・正心法語』『祈願文①』『祈願文②』『エル・カンターレへの祈り』が授与されます。

植福の会

植福は、ユートピア建設のために、自分の富を差し出す尊い布施の行為です。布施の機会として、毎月1口1,000円からお申込みいただける、「植福の会」がございます。

ご希望の方には、幸福の科学の小冊子（毎月1回）をお送りいたします。詳しくは、下記の電話番号までお問い合わせください。

月刊「幸福の科学」

ザ・伝道

ヤング・ブッダ

ヘルメス・エンゼルズ

INFORMATION

幸福の科学サービスセンター
TEL. 03-5793-1727 （受付時間 火～金：10～20時／土・日：10～18時）
幸福の科学 公式サイト **happy-science.jp**